# THE GREAT COMPOSERS
### THEIR LIVES AND TIMES

Modest
# *Mussorgsky*
**1839-1881**

Nikolay
# *Rimsky-Korsakov*
**1844-1908**

Sergei
# *Rachmaninov*
**1873-1943**

Sergei
# *Prokofiev*
**1891-1953**

Dmitri
# *Shostakovich*
**1906-1975**

# THE GREAT COMPOSERS
## THEIR LIVES AND TIMES

Modest
# *Mussorgsky*
### 1839-1881

Nikolay
# *Rimsky–Korsakov*
### 1844-1908

Sergei
# *Rachmaninov*
### 1873-1943

Sergei
# *Prokofiev*
### 1891-1953

Dmitri
# *Shostakovich*
### 1906-1975

**MARSHALL CAVENDISH**
**NEW YORK · LONDON · SYDNEY**

# Staff Credits

**Editors**
*Laura Buller*
*David Buxton*

**Art Editors**
*Helen James*
*Debbie Jecock*

**Deputy Editor**
*Barbara Segall*

**Sub-editors**
*Geraldine Jones*
*Judy Oliver*
*Nigel Rodgers*

**Designers**
*Steve Chilcott*
*Shirin Patel*
*Chris Rathbone*

**Picture Researchers**
*Georgina Barker*
*Julia Calloway*
*Vanessa Cawley*

**Production Controllers**
*Deborah Cracknell*
*Sue Fuller*

**Secretary**
*Lynn Small*

**Publishing Director**
*Reg Wright*

**Managing Editor**
*Sue Lyon*

**Consultants**
*Dr Antony Hopkins*
*Commander of the Order*
*of the British Empire*
*Fellow of the*
*Royal College of Music*

*Nick Mapstone BA, MA*

*Keith Shadwick BA*

**Reference Edition Published 1990**

*Published by Marshall Cavendish Corporation*
*147 West Merrick Road*
*Freeport, Long Island*
*N.Y. 11520*

*Typeset by Maclink, Hull*
*Printed by Times Offset Private Ltd.,*
*Singapore*

© *Marshall Cavendish Limited MCMLXXXIV,*
*MCMLXXXVII, MCMXC*

**Library of Congress Cataloging-in-Publication Data**

*The Composers: the great composers, their lives and times.*
   *p. ca.*
   *Cover title: Great composers II.*
   *ISBN 1-85435-300-4 (set): $175.00*
   *1. Composers—Biography.   2. Music appreciation.*
*I. Marshall Cavendish Corporation.*
*II. Title: Great composers II.*
*ML390.C7185 1990   780'.92'2—dc20 [B]   89-23988*

*ISBN 1-85435-300-4 (set)                       CIP*
   *1-85435-303-9 (vol)                          MN*

THE
# GREAT COMPOSERS
THEIR LIVES AND TIMES

# Contents

# Introduction

Before Peter the Great opened his 'window to the West', Russia was for the most part musically insular. No Russian composers had achieved international standing, the availability of formal music training was limited, and the Russian Orthodox Church banned the use of musical instruments. But social and political changes in the latter half of the 18th century brought about many musical breakthroughs: the growth of music publishing, early developments in music education, the establishment of major theatres in St. Petersburg and Moscow, exposure to French and Italian operas, the first collections of Russian folk songs, and the growth of instrumental music. By the 1850s, these 'firsts' were firmly consolidated, giving rise to the development of diverse but distinctly Russian music by the composers found in this volume.

In St. Petersburg, a group of composers known as the 'Mighty Handful' emerged. Led by Mily Alexeyevich Balakirev, these composers were dedicated to expressing a national, rather than an individual, identity in their music. Two members of the group in particular – Modest Mussorgsky and Nikolay Rimsky-Korsakov – composed powerful and colourful works which helped to raise the international status of Russian music. Russia's new generation of composers enjoyed the benefits of this musical sophistication, exploring more individual styles of composition. Sergei Rachmaninov's rich works and his virtuoso piano skills earned international acclaim. Sergei Prokofiev and Dmitri Shostakovich both wrote remarkable music in a bold, modern style, profoundly shaping 20th-century music.

## THE GREAT COMPOSERS

# Modest Mussorgsky

### (1839–1881)

*In the vanguard of the Nationalist movement in 19th century Russia came the 'Mighty Handful', a group of composers who shared the common ideal of expressing a sense of national pride and belonging. The group was comprised of Balakirev, their musical mentor, Cui, Borodin, Rimsky-Korsakov and Modest Mussorgsky, whose absolute dedication to the cause of Russian music made him the group's spiritual leader. Meeting with Balakirev in St. Petersburg, the group interchanged ideas and musical compositions. Drawing on Spanish, Oriental and Russian peasant themes, the works analysed in the* Listener's Guide *(Borodin's Polovtsian Dances, Mussorgsky's Night on a Bare Mountain and Rimsky-Korsakov's Easter Overture and Capriccio Espagnol) are all stamped with Russian colour. Reforms following Russia's defeat in the Crimean War, examined in* In the Background, *gave new inspiration to its nationalist composers, whose works shaped the course of Russian music.*

*Modest Mussorgsky saw as his life's task to 'bring the past into the present' with his powerful compositions based on Russian themes. Born in the village of Karevo, he was a gifted pianist as a child. He attended cadet school in St. Petersburg, but his father encouraged his interest in music by paying for the publishing of his first work in 1852. As an army lieutenant in 1856, he met Borodin, who encouraged his musical growth; in 1858, Mussorgsky resigned his commission to study with Balakirev. A new period of creativity followed, although Mussorgsky was often hampered by the damaging physical effects of alcoholism. Within the nationalist ideals of the 'Mighty Handful', he wrote his greatest work, Boris Godunov, completed in 1872. Despite his success, however, Mussorgsky lived in despondency; he left works unfinished, his relationships soured, and his alcoholism worsened. He died in 1881.*

*The members of 'The Mighty Handful' (centre, then clockwise from left): Modest Petrovich Mussorgsky; Alexander Porfir'yevich Borodin; César Antonovich Cui; Nikolay Andreyevich Rimsky-Korsakov; and Mily Alexeyevich Balakirev.*

## COMPOSER'S LIFE

# 'The Mighty Handful'

*Nationalist music began in Russia with the work of five composers known as 'The Mighty Handful'. Of these, the gifted but tragic Mussorgsky came closest to illuminating the Russian soul.*

In the middle of the 19th century Russian music, aside from folk music, did not exist as an entity. What there was was modelled on European counterparts, with the Conservatoire in Moscow serving as the arbiter of musical acceptability.

Glinka, perhaps Russia's best known composer at the time, saw a desperate need for a school of nationalist music and he struck a sympathetic chord in another influential composer, Dargomĭzhsky. But it was not until five young composers got together, argued, listened and played to each other their music, that these ambitions were finally realised.

The putative leader of 'The Five' (or 'The Mighty Handful', a term coined by the music critic Vladimir Stasov) was Balakirev (1837–1910). A strict tutor and an uncompromising theoretician, he laid the technical ground rules for the group. César Cui (1835–1918), although a mediocre composer, considered himself joint leader and group critic. Borodin (1833–87) was both a composer and a chemist with an international reputation. His musical output was small, but it contained some masterpieces. Rimsky-Korsakov (1844–1908), though he too had a dual role as a composer and naval officer, maintained a staggering output of compositions and orchestrations. Though his commitment to the group's ideals was sometimes called into question he was, nevertheless, one of its mainstays. Mussorgsky was the black sheep of the group, but also its spiritual dynamo, and his music states loudest of all their manifesto.

## The young Mussorgsky

Modest Petrovich Mussorgsky was born on 21 March 1839 in the small village of Karevo, the fourth of four sons. Mussorgsky's father, though the son of a peasant girl, owned 27,000 acres of land and the family was comfortably off. Little is known of Mussorgsky's childhood; the autobiographical sketches he wrote a year before his death are somewhat inaccurate. But undoubtedly he was exposed to folk songs and stories during his formative years, and later these inspired one of his important contributions to The Five's aims: to accurately portray speech in music. Encouraged by his mother Julia to practise the piano, Mussorgsky gained enough facility to perform a concerto before a large audience in the family home when he was only nine.

Mussorgsky's family intended that he pursue a military career, and in 1849 he was enrolled at the Peter and Paul School in St Petersburg to prepare him for the School for Cadets of the Guards. During this time he had piano lessons from Anton Herke, a brilliant virtuoso, who introduced him to the work of Schumann. In 1851 Mussorgsky achieved his first public success when he was rewarded for playing a *rondo* at a charity function with a copy of Beethoven's Sonata in A flat. In the same year he changed schools to study for the Cadets' School entrance examination.

At the Cadets' School the young Mussorgsky found himself in charge of a man-servant whom, had he so wished, he could have beaten on a whim. In a place where the senior boys could command the juniors to carry them piggy-back to the washstands and where womanizing and drunkenness – providing it was on champagne and not vodka – was openly encouraged, Mussorgsky was seen as a bit of a disappointment as he pored over tomes of German philosophy and history. He learned no music theory, nor was he exposed to the work of Glinka and Dargomĭzhsky.

*'A perfectly contrived little officer (with) signs of a slight pretentiousness' was how Borodin described Mussorgsky (right) at their first meeting in 1856 when Mussorgsky was 17. At the time Mussorgsky was in the Preobrajensky Regiment, having completed his military education at the St Petersburg School for Cadets of the Guards. Though his parents intended that he should follow a military career, Mussorgsky kept up his musical studies while at military school, and eventually resigned his commission.*

*Mussorgsky arrived in St Petersburg (below) aged 13 to begin his military studies. Although stimulated by his sophisticated surroundings the inspiration for his music came from his peasant origins.*

J. V. Chelminski 'A Winter's day in St. Petersburg' Archiv für Kunst und Geschichte

Society for Cultural Relations with the USSR

Novosti

*The music critic Vladimir Stasov (above) coined the name 'The Mighty Handful'. From his Russian homeland (below), Mussorgsky drew inspiration for his most colourful music.*

widened his musical circle to include, via an introduction to Dargomïzhsky, Balakirev, Cui and Stasov, and nurtured serious composing ambitions. The type of music the budding group was formulating would have fallen on unsympathetic ears, for the St Petersburg public wanted Italian opera, not the music of mother Russia. During this period Mussorgsky also developed a taste for alcohol — one which he never mastered.

### The beginnings of nationalist music

Glinka's death in 1857 did little to curtail the development of nationalist music; a more serious impediment, however, was the lack of facilities: there were few places to study technique, few books and fewer teachers. Composers had to pool their resources and knowledge, and thus it was inevitable that Mussorgsky, Balakirev and the others would join forces.

Though Balakirev was the younger, he became Mussorgsky's tutor. A hard taskmaster, he made

A. Saurasov 'The Rooks have arrived'. Society for Cultural Relations with the USSR

Nevertheless he did delight his comrades by singing and playing popular pieces, and it was to them that he dedicated his first published work in 1852 — a polka.

In 1856, at 17, Mussorgsky entered the Pre-obrajensky Regiment as an ensign. In the same year he met Borodin who was six years his senior. Borodin recalled the occasion:

*Mussorgsky was, at that time, a very callow, most elegant, perfectly contrived little officer: brand-new close fitting uniform, toes well turned out, hair well oiled and carefully smoothed out, hands shapely and well cared for . . . He showed, in fact, signs of a slight pretentiousness; but also, quite unmistakably, of perfect breeding and education. He sat down at the piano, and coquettishly raising his hands, started playing, delicately and gracefully . . .*

Alexander Borodin was at this time a house surgeon at a military hospital; he was prodigiously well educated, gifted in both science and music and, although only 23, had an established international scientific reputation. No wonder, then, that Mussorgsky seemed like a callow youth! When they met again in the autumn of 1862 Borodin slightly revised his first opinion: 'He had grown more virile, and was beginning to put on flesh,' he wrote. 'His attire, his manners, were as dainty as ever, but no trace of foppishness remained.' The two played Mendelssohn's A minor Symphony together and Borodin began to gain an idea of Mussorgsky's musical growth during the intervening years. These years had been crucial for Mussorgsky: he had

*From the age of eight, encouraged by his mother, Alexander Borodin (left) showed a great enthusiasm for music. In his early teens he also developed an interest in chemistry, in which field he spent most of his working life.*

community. Each member had his own room and there was a single common room where together they discussed ways of putting the world right. To fund himself, he joined the civil service with the rank of collegiate secretary at the Central Engineering Board. Like Borodin he had to divide his time between music and a profession, but Mussorgsky derived no satisfaction from his dull office routine.

Life in the commune was characterized by a lack of hygiene, a poor diet and the consumption of vast amounts of alcohol. Mussorgsky's system, already weakened by over-indulgence during his military days, could not take it and in the autumn of 1865 he succumbed to a fit of delirium tremens. While recovering at the house of his brother Philaret, he struck up a close friendship with Rimsky-Korsakov who had, as a naval officer, just returned from a world cruise.

With their friendship the group moved closer to having a recognizable identity. A further step was taken when Lyudmila Shastakova, a woman who passionately supported the new Russian music, offered open house to like-minded musicians and scholars. The Five plus Vladimir Stasov and his brother Dimitri found a congenial forum there and Mussorgsky, in Lyudmila, a staunch and loyal ally.

### The productive years

During the period 1866–69 the group interacted at fever pitch, as Lyudmila recounted: 'The days were not long enough for them to play all their new works to one another, and talk music. So, after leaving my house, loth to part company, they would spend

Mussorgsky play all of Beethoven's symphonies at the piano and then analyze their structure. It was under Balakirev's inflexible and dictatorial guidance that Mussorgsky began to realise his own genius, and in 1858 he resigned his commission to devote himself to music. During that summer Mussorgsky had a nervous breakdown and took the waters at Tikhvin but this did not totally undermine his growing self-confidence,

In 1856, a deep-rooted feeling of oneness with Russia blossomed in Mussorgsky when he took a trip through the country. He wrote to Balakirev, 'You know I have been a cosmopolitan, but now I have undergone a sort of rebirth: I have been brought near to everything Russian.' His first public performance came in the following year: his *Scherzo* in B flat, conducted by Anton Rubinstein, was well received. A further nervous crisis occurred during the summer months of 1860, however, and it was not until the autumn that he felt sufficiently recovered to embark on a new period of creativity.

By 1863 Borodin had met and married a brilliant pianist, Ekaterina Protopopova, and had taken quarters in the laboratory of the Medico-Surgical Academy; the couple were to remain there until Borodin's death in 1887. Mussorgsky's lifestyle, meanwhile, was that of an intellectual tearaway. In the autumn of 1863 he joined a small, all-male

*Borodin first attended the Medico-Surgical Academy (above) in St Petersburg as a student in 1850. When he graduated in 1856 it was with great honour and he was appointed assistant in general pathology and therapy. In the subsequent years he spent much time abroad, presenting papers and generally continuing his studies. In 1892 he returned to St Petersburg and was appointed reader in chemistry at the Academy. He became professor of chemistry there in 1864.*

much time escorting one another home.'

In April 1867 Mussorgsky lost his job because of a reorganization in the department, but this did not depress him. Indeed, colourful and witty songs like *The Urchin, The He-Goat* and *Gathering Mushrooms,* each a cameo of Russian life, poured from him. He finished the score of *A Night on the Bare Mountain* in 12 days, commenting: 'My music is Russian and independent in form and character, fiery and disorderly in tone . . . I see in this wicked prank of mine a really Russian and original achievement, quite free from German profundity and routine.'

His friendship with Rimsky-Korsakov – though later to go through a rough patch – deepened between 1867 and 1874. Together with Borodin they saw themselves as the juniors of The Five, with Balakirev and Cui dictating and them obeying. The three often met at Lyudmila's and she observed their curious artistic relationship. Rimsky-Korsakov would sit at the piano and play his latest achievement, after which Mussorgsky offered his comments, while Rimsky-Korsakov would pace up and down the room. Mussorgsky would remain quietly seated, or play bits on the piano, until Rimsky-Korsakov regained his composure, came close to him and listened attentively to his talk, and then ended by agreeing.

The group had a productive year in 1868. Borodin took up work on *Prince Igor;* Balakirev was busy with *The Fire-Bird,* an opera he had been planning for five years; Cui was putting the finishing touches on *Ratcliff;* Rimsky-Korsakov started on *The Maid of*

*In the summer of 1869, Borodin began work on the libretto and music for his opera* Prince Igor, *which 18 years later – at his death – was still unfinished and largely unorchestrated.* Prince Igor, *(title page shown below), was completed and the orchestration finished by Rimsky-Korsakov and Glazunov. The first performance was given at the Mariinsky Theatre in 1890. The set (left) for the prologue to the opera was designed for the 1934 Bolshoi production in Moscow and the costumes (below right) were for an earlier production in 1914.*

*Pskov;* and Mussorgsky began work on his masterpiece, the opera *Boris Godunov,* with his own libretto based partly on Pushkin's play. The opera was later mounted in various versions, with the great opera singer Fyodor Shalyapin in the leading role. His performance inspired many imitators.

It was a good year in other ways for Mussorgsky. He found a pleasant home with some old friends and in December he was made assistant head clerk in the Forestry Department. Things seemed to be looking up. The flurry of letters he wrote to his friends at this time show the importance to him of their approval. The letters also reveal the intense interaction between The Five as they hammered out a set of parameters to govern not just their musical development, but their own personal philosophies. For Mussorgsky this meant 'finding one's own self'.

The foundations of the edifice The Five had been building trembled when, in January 1869, Dargomīzhsky—'the great teacher of musical truth' as Mussorgsky saw him—died. It fell to Cui and Rimsky-Korsakov to finish his *The Stone Guest.* When it was performed it met with as little enthusiasm as Cui's *Ratcliff,* in which he had tried to embody the ideals of the group in his own pedestrian fashion. In the same year Balakirev had to give up his post as conductor of the Russian Music Society for not toeing the official line and showing disdain towards the Conservatoire. Mussorgsky revealed a hidden talent for satire in writing a piece called *The Peep Show* – a musical lampoon on the Conservatoire's staff and supporters. At the end of the year he was promoted to the rank of collegiate assessor, a job that brought little advancement and even more tedium.

In the autumn of 1871 Mussorgsky and Rimsky-Korsakov, in order to come into closer artistic contact, decided to share a room. It contained a piano and a writing table. Mussorgsky had the use of the piano until noon, when he had to go to his office, while Rimsky-Korsakov sat writing. As for the evenings they 'made arrangements according to circumstance'. Borodin thought it was an excellent idea: 'Both have considerably improved since they started sharing a room,' he wrote.

A marvellous opportunity arose in 1871 when four of The Five – Mussorgsky, Borodin, Cui and Rimsky-Korsakov – were commissioned by the Director of the Imperial Theatres to set to music his libretto for a

*In 1868 Mussorgsky began work on his masterpiece – an opera on the subject of Pushkin's play* **Boris Godunov** *(above). He wrote his own libretto and the opera was first performed at the Mariinsky Theatre on 8 February 1874 with the great opera singer Fyodor Shalyapin (below) in the title role.*

ballet opera called *Mlada*. Each composer was to write one act. Mussorgsky was not flattered, nor was Rimsky-Korsakov, but neither of them wanted to stand in the way of Cui or Borodin, who were enthusiastic about the project. However, *Mlada* was never completed.

### The demise of The Five

The demise of The Five began during the *Mlada* period and affected Mussorgsky badly. Perhaps he saw in this the end of a moral support which had restrained his drinking and shored up his shaky self-confidence. He began to see himself as a lone crusader on the road to 'the true, the luminous goal, towards the true art that loves humanity, living all its joys, pains and labours'.

By 1873 Mussorgsky was indulging his craving for alcohol to the full. Thin and sullen, he would sell his clothes and furniture to go drinking in cheap taverns where Vladimir Stasov would eventually find him mindlessly drunk.

Two other things may have put him on a downward path that year: one was the death at 39 of the painter and architect Victor Hartmann, who was a very dear friend – Mussorgsky would later pay a tribute to his memory in his piano suite *Pictures at an Exhibition*. The other was the departure of

Rimsky-Korsakov from their shared accommodation upon his marriage; to Mussorgsky this represented the loss of another prop.

When his great friend Nadejda Opotchinina died in June 1874 at only 53 Mussorgsky's powers of concentration were weakened. He put down *Khovanshchina* and took up *The Sorotchintsi Fair*, and then began working on them side by side. It was a mistake: he never finished either of them. And he took to the bottle again with a vengeance. He would spend whole nights drinking hard at the Malo-Yaroslavets restaurant, alone or with new acquaintances, and when playing and singing to the aristocratic circles that he sometimes moved in, he was further plied with drink. His energy was dissipated while his health deteriorated.

Somehow he managed to do his office work and was even promoted to senior head clerk, but his relationship with The Five soured. He considered that with Balakirev relaxing his iron grip, the others were sliding back into traditional music.

### Mussorgsky's last years

Mussorgsky meanwhile lurched along his own path to ruin. Turned out of his flat for not paying the rent, he wandered the streets with a few possessions in a bag and eventually ended up on the doorstep of a

and sounds that assailed his senses rejuvenated him: 'Years have fallen from my shoulders, life is calling me to new musical tasks, to grand musical doings.' Sadly he was deluding himself.

When it became obvious that he and the government service would soon have to part company, some friends clubbed together to provide an allowance so that he could finish *Khovanshchina*. Another well-meaning group was formed to pay him to complete *The Sorotchintsi Fair*. He made very little progress with either opera, though he convinced himself otherwise.

Shabbily dressed in second-hand clothes and looking much older than his 41 years, he made a sad figure. Most of his friends had deserted him, though Darya Leonova stood by him, and with her he organized a singing school to which he devoted much of his remaining time. What he earned he drank, thus bringing on his final collapse in February 1881. After suffering what appeared to be an epileptic fit at a garden party, he was persuaded by Stasov and Filippov to go to hospital.

A few days before his death he said, 'All is well now. I am cured, and shall soon be able to resume work.' On Monday 16 March he cried out: 'All is over: Woe is me!' and died. The cause of death was given as erysipelous inflammation of the legs, but cirrhosis of the liver and a bottle of brandy smuggled to him by one of the hospital staff were no doubt contributory factors. An impressive funeral took place on 18 March, with wreaths sent from the Imperial Theatres and the Conservatoire. Four years later a monument to him was unveiled. It bore the inscription: 'And thus the future generations/Will of their faith and people learn the past.' Mussorgsky would have been pleased to know that the corners of the veil were held by the four survivors of The Five.

*Mussorgsky paid tribute to the art of his dead friend Victor Hartmann in the work* **Pictures at an Exhibition.** *The seventh item in this musical record of a visit to the exhibition was Hartmann's representation (left) of himself and a friend being shown the Paris catacombs.*

friend, Paul Naumof, who lived, to polite society's horror, with his sister-in-law. The two of them seemed to understand him better than most and he was happy there – so happy he stayed for four years!

Stasov recognised that Mussorgsky's days in the department were numbered: he helped to have him transferred to the Government Control Department which was run by his friend Filippov. Filippov, an ardent admirer of Mussorgsky's work, was wholly indulgent to the composer's 'nervous disorder', even when he arrived at the office tottering. Soon after the transfer Mussorgsky suffered what seemed like an alcohol induced stroke, but such were his powers of recovery that a month later he attended the 20th performance of *Boris Godunov* at the Mariinsky Theatre, taking several calls.

In the late spring of 1879 Darya Leonova, a faded contralto of 50, suggested to Mussorgsky that he tour central and south Russia with her as accompanist. The group considered this a vulgar and shameless thing to even contemplate, but Filippov readily granted Mussorgsky three months' leave.

An opera singer past her prime and an alcoholic accompanist could have meant disaster, but in many ways for Mussorgsky the trip was a success. He didn't make the 1000 rouble profit he was hoping for and the audiences were sometimes sparse, but the sights

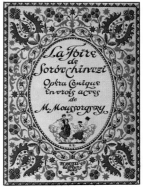

Mauro Pucciarelli

***Many of Mussorgsky's compositions including his comic opera* The Sorotchintsi Fair *(title page above) were completed after his death by Rimsky-Korsakov and others. Mussorgsky (right), painted a few weeks before his death in the Nikolayevsky Military Hospital.***

Repin 'Modest Mussorgsky' Novosti

# A Russian festival

*Through mighty composers like Borodin, Mussorgsky and Rimsky-Korsakov, Russia produced a carnival of colourful music, European in flavour yet spiced with distinctively national folk themes.*

The group of disciples who met with Balakirev for musical guidance in St. Petersburg, around 1861, were destined to be dubbed 'The Mighty Handful' ('moguchaya kuchka') by the critic Stasov in 1867. In the years between they had become a force to be reckoned with and, despite busy and varied careers, they had managed to redirect the entire course of Russian music. It is often said that the government, military and academic careers of this 'Handful' – Balakirev, Cui, Mussorgsky, Borodin and Rimsky-Korsakov – kept them in touch with major European trends in music while they were cultivating a so-called 'Russian' style (incorporating folk-tune elements and colourful instrumental effects). A list of their international composer friends reads like a Who's Who of musical greats at that time: Tchaikovsky, Liszt, Saint-Saëns, Berlioz and so on. Although they did use Russian history and legend for their source material, they also ranged through the wealth of European culture: Shakespeare, Flaubert, Heine, Byron, Goethe, Hugo, Dumas, Maupassant, Mérimée – all provided inspiration for song texts and opera librettos.

Among the members of the 'Handful', it was the youngest of the group – Rimsky-Korsakov (who was nearest in age to Tchaikovsky), who explored colourful orchestration to the full. Not only a brilliant musician, he was also an outstandingly loyal friend. After the deaths of Dargomïzhsky, Mussorgsky and Borodin, it was Rimsky who completed and publicised their works. It is, therefore, appropriate that his orchestrations are described on the following pages.

## Borodin: Polovtsian Dances

The great musical project of Borodin's life was, undoubtedly, his vast epic opera Prince Igor. Like most of the Nationalist group, he aimed at a work to continue in the tradition of *Ivan Susanin* and *Rusland and Lyudmila* (operas by Glinka). He had started work on *The Czar's Bride* but, by 1869, was unhappy with the results and making poor progress. Then, on April 30, the critic Stasov sent him an outline of an opera based on the medieval Russian epic *Slovo o polku Igoreve* (the story of Igor's army). Borodin insisted on both com-

posing and writing his own libretto, which eventually emerged as a prologue and four acts – a massive work worthy of the highly esteemed German operatic composer Meyerbeer (1791–1864).

Unfortunately, Borodin's academic post as professor of chemistry, together with his many other commitments, left him little time for composition. It was Rimsky-Korsakov, always an energizing force among his friends, who drove Borodin onwards. In the summer of 1875 he managed to compose the Polovtsian Dances. But Rimsky still had to nag him to get them orchestrated in time for a concert on 11 March 1879!

Rimsky himself writes about the frustration of waiting endlessly to receive an orchestration from Borodin. The numbers had already been announced and rehearsed with the chorus, but the parts had not been copied out. He heaped reproaches on his friend and finally, in desperation, offered to help with the task. Thankfully, Borodin came round to his house one evening, bringing with him the outline score of the Polovtsian Dances. With the further assistance of Anatoli Lyadov, the three men set about their work in haste. Rimsky's description of the scene continues:

*To gain time, we wrote in pencil and not in ink. Thus we sat at work until late at night. The finished sheets of the score Borodin covered with liquid gelatine, to keep our pencil marks intact, and in order to have the sheets dry the sooner, he hung them out like washing on lines in my study. Thus the number was ready and passed on to the copyist'.*

Despite all their efforts, and the success of the concerts, which also included excerpts from Mussorgsky and Rimsky-Korsakov, Borodin did not complete the opera. Rimsky and Glazunov undertook its completion and it is their version that has become a permanent part of the repertoire in the Soviet Union.

## Programme notes

The plot of the opera can be briefly summarized as follows: Prince Igor, ruler of Putivle, takes his son Vladimir with his army to meet an attack by the raiding Polovtsi – a mongol tribe led by the powerful Khan Kontchak. Igor leaves his young wife Yaroslavna in the care of his

Degas 'Two Russian Dancers'

*A Russian epic on a Mongolian theme was the source of inspiration for Borodin's exuberant Polovtsian dances. Brash, colourful orchestration conjures up an atmosphere of oriental splendour, although the spirit and vitality of the dances is entirely Russian in idiom (left).*

brother-in-law Galitsky. Despite an ominous eclipse of the sun, and the desperate pleading of his wife, Igor departs. Galitsky takes advantage of Igor's absence to live a life of decadent pleasure. The horrified wife braves his insults only giving way to despair when she hears that both Igor and Vladimir have been captured and the army defeated. In the midst of her grief, another tribe of Polovtsi attacks the defenceless city.

In Act II, Igor is entertained by Khan Kontchak, who wants Igor to become his ally and help him conquer all of Russia; Vladimir has been seduced by the Khan's daughter. The Polovtsian Dances are performed with choruses and dancers in the opera, but in concert versions, the vocal parts are effectively assigned to orchestral instruments. The dances combine seductive charm with an underlying barbarity — a contrast which is the essential theme of the opera. Igor eventually realizes that he must escape and somehow stop the mighty Khan. He is forced to leave Vladimir behind with the Khan's daughter. The opera ends as Igor is reunited with his wife and they both join in the hopeful celebrations among the ruins of Putivle.

The dances which are, incidentally, in a slightly different order in operatic versions, display the oriental splendour of the Khan's court. At his command, male and female slaves enter with drums and other instruments. During the following scene, men, women, young boys and girls join in, dancing ever more wildly. The scurrying theme of the dance of young boys is played on the woodwind and is

*Contrasting with the wildness and barbarism of the opening dances, is the seductive dance of the young girls. This features a theme which evokes all the languid charm of the harem (below), and is famous as the source of the song Stranger in Paradise.*

Severo Etchart 'Ladies of the Harem'. Mathaf Gallery, Motcomb St., London SW1

repeated with the addition of drums and cymbals in a very lively dance rhythm.

The dance of the young girls follows. (In the opera, it is accompanied by a women's chorus singing a song of longing for a homeland far away.) The introductory melody appears on the flute and is then taken up by clarinet and oboe. The main theme is then stated: lovers of Broadway musicals will immediately recognize the source of the song 'Take my hand, I'm a stranger in Paradise', which appears in *Kismet*. This famous melody is restated by the strings of the orchestra, while a harp adds to the exotic colour.

The oriental flavour of the Dance of the Men is accentuated by the balance of drum and flute. Flute and piccolo carry the melody while a throbbing percussion accompaniment is soon decorated by brass, cymbals and triangle.

The General Dance which concludes the ballet, is a song of glory to Khan Kontchak in the operatic version. Trombones and an explosion of percussion — a giant tam-tam is used — depict the orgiastic celebrations. A central section scored for strings, flute and triangle represents the Dance of the Girl Slaves (in the opera, Kontchak tries to tempt Igor with the offer of one of them). The wild general dance returns. A brilliant merging of all the dances occurs in the finale. The Boys' Dance, with its busy string figures and *pizzicata* (plucked) accompaniment blends with the Men's Dance and bold statements by the brass. The Women's tune reappears and is then joined to the dance of praise for the Khan. The rising frenzy is shown in the complex orchestral colour — especially the use of a bass tuba as a drone under the drums, trombones, cymbals, triangle and assorted brass. The thunderous conclusion gives the perfect picture of barbaric display through magnificent orchestration.

## Rimsky-Korsakov: Easter Overture

During the summer of 1888, Rimsky-Korsakov finished both *Scheherazade* and *The Bright Holiday,* an Easter Overture based on the canticles of the Greek Orthodox Church. In his autobiography, *My Musical Life,* Rimsky outlines what he was attempting in his overture.

The piece starts with a lengthy, slow introduction on the theme of 'Let God Arise', alternating with another ecclesiastical theme, 'An angel wailed'. This solemn mood is then replaced by the holiday mood of Easter Sunday; the trumpet voice of the Archangel is replaced by sounds of the church service — bells

*The sombre opening of Rimsky-Korsakov's Russian Easter Overture suggests a solemn religious procession (above). For the composer, such liturgical themes provided a powerful stimulus: 'Do not the waving beards of the priests clad in white vestments and surplices . . . transport the imagination to pagan times?'*

ringing, a priest chanting — before the merry-making proper begins.

*This legendary and heathen side of the holiday, this transition from the gloomy and mysterious evening of Passion Saturday to the unbridled pagan-religious merry-making on the morn of Easter Sunday, is what I was eager to reproduce.*

## Programme notes

The trombone acts as cantor announcing the Easter service at the beginning of the Overture. A plucked string accompaniment is added, followed by a virtuoso solo section for violin. The liturgical theme recurs on the flute, is restated by the tuba and echoed by the strings. Flute and clarinet then introduce the second theme, carefully balanced with the violinist. Bassoons, cellos, harp and shimmering strings lead to a more insistent interpretation of this second theme. The central passage of the overture appears in violent conflict with the jagged variation repeated by the brass and overlaid with strings:

Example 1

Trumpets return again and again, each time with new orchestral colouring interweaving the two themes. Flutes, piccolo, oboes, clarinets, bassoons, horns, kettle-drums, glockenspiel, triangle, cymbals, bass drum, strings and harp: all help to display Rimsky's orchestral virtuosity. The

*In a splash of colour, the subdued mood is transformed into one of 'unbridled pagan-religious merry-making' (below). The trumpet of the Archangel heralds the dawn of Easter Sunday, while the angels sing out 'RESURREXIT.'*

composer's own programme notes to the piece explain the triumphant conclusion: 'RESURREXIT!' sing the chorus of angels in Heaven to the sound of the Archangels' trumpets and the fluttering of the wings of the seraphim. 'RESURREXIT!' sing the priests in the temples in the midst of clouds of incense, by the light of innumerable candles, to the chiming of triumphant bells.'

According to Rimsky, it was only possible to fully appreciate his Overture if the listener had attended an Easter morning service 'in a cathedral thronged with people from every walk of life, with several priests conducting the service'. Not surprisingly, this comment was 'censored' by the Soviet editors of his autobiography.

*The ornate title page to the Russian Easter Overture (right).*

## Mussorgsky: A Night on the Bare Mountain

Mussorgsky left so many works unfinished or in disorder that, at his death, it was a great temptation for Rimsky-Korsakov to edit both finished and unfinished works in rather cavalier fashion. In the case of *Bare Mountain,* for example, Mussorgsky left a perfectly performable orchestral version, completed in 1867, yet it is the Rimsky-Korsakov version of 1886 that is most often used. Rimsky described his friend's work as 'new and vital', but still rewrote and corrected the original score.

### Programme notes

Mussorgsky finished the composition on 23rd June (St. John's Night) – the night of the Witches' Sabbath described so dramatically in his music. In a letter to Rimsky, he describes the programme:

*(1) assembly of the witches, their chatter and hubbub; (2) Satan's pageant; (3) unholy glorification of Satan; and (4) witches' sabbath. I wrote the score just like that, without any preliminary rough draft—I began on the tenth day of June, and by the twenty-third there was joy and triumph.*

In writing to another friend (Nikolsky) he

*Mussorgsky's* **Night on a Bare Mountain** *is a dark, sinister work, dynamically orchestrated by Rimsky-Korsakov. It opens ominously with the 'subterranean din of supernatural voices' heralding the start of a witches' sabbath (below left). As the black mass gets more and more frenzied, chatters and shrieks pierce the darkness. Then the bells of the village church ring and, as the evil spirits disperse, dawn breaks over the dismal landscape (right).*

also refers to a 'scattered but continuous cross-fire of calls, until the whole rabble unite in the final embrace'.

The Rimsky version is dynamic and colourful and bears his own outline of his rescoring:

*Subterranean din of supernatural voices. Appearance of the Spirits of Darkness, followed by that of Tschernobog – Glorification of the Black God. The black mass – the Witches' Sabbath. At the height of the revelry, the bell of a village church sounds in the distance, whereupon the spirits of darkness disperse – Dawn breaks.*

The piece is a tour de force for the strings,

*Caspar David Friedrich 'Mountain Landscape with Mist'. Neue Pinakothek, Munich. Joachim Blauel/Artothek*

who are given difficult, whirling melodic lines. The woodwinds alternately chatter and shriek, while a powerful line is pounded out on the trombones. The witches' dancing seems to be portrayed in the following theme:

Example 2

At this stage, the work becomes a series of disjointed variations on the main themes

and the orgy grows wilder and wilder. Dance sections between the fanfares have slavonic harmonies – making these decidedly Russian witches! Nonetheless, this piece is linked to the kind of 'Dance of Death' made popular by Liszt and the German romantics. Saint-Saéns, too, made a contribution with his *Danse Macabre* of 1874.

Suddenly, bells are heard in the distance as dawn approaches and the furore dies away. Wistful rising string figures indicate the evil spirits drifting away. Harp arpeggios accompany a plaintive passage for a solo clarinet and then another for solo flute as the Sabbath is dispelled by the morning sun.

## Rimsky-Korsakov: Capriccio Espagnol

The Spanish Capriccio was composed in 1887 after the orchestration of *Prince Igor* and just before the Easter Festival Overture and *Scheherazade.* Like Mussorgsky and Borodin, Rimsky delighted in colourful and effective orchestration, and claimed Glinka as a great influence on him. In his own words, the Spanish Capriccio, the Easter Festival and *Scheherazade* 'closed a period of my work, at the end of which my orchestration had attained a considerable degree of virtuosity and warm sonority without Wagnerian influence . . .' Even at this late stage in his

# *Understanding music: the late-Romantic orchestra*

During the second half of the 19th century, late-Romantic self expression, which found one of its outlets in the Nationalist school, prompted the development of an enlarged, more flexible symphony orchestra. The orchestra had already begun to expand to match the large-scale works conceived for it, such as the *Grande messe des morts* (Requiem) of Berlioz, while Wagner's music dramas with their boldly imaginative chromatic harmony were revolutionary in impact and demanded orchestration of new flexibility and density.

Berlioz's treatise *Grand traité d'instrumentation et d'orchestration modernes* (1843) was widely read and the influence of both Berlioz and Wagner was felt by almost all later composers. Rimsky-Korsakov, too, wrote a highly-influential treatise on orchestration and pointed out in his *Capriccio Espagnol* that its brilliant instrumental colouring was 'the very essence of the composition, not its mere dressing-up'.

At the same time, a search for colourful and exotic effects brought new uses of instruments such as muted brass in Rimsky-Korsakov's *Scheherazade* and Strauss's *Till Eulenspiegel,* and even new or unfamiliar instruments like the bass flute in Rimsky-Korsakov's *Mlada,* the celeste and bass clarinet in Tchaikovsky's *Nutcracker,* the saxophone in Bizet's *L'Arlésienne,* the cor anglais (English horn) and the harp in Berlioz's *Symphonie Fantastique* and the cymbals in Debussy's *Prélude à l'après midi d'un faune.* Wagner himself, dissatisfied with the resources of the traditional symphony orchestra, introduced the 'Wagner tubas' and a double-bass tuba in the 'Ring', as well as a bass trumpet. His orchestra for this mighty work included triple woodwind – with piccolo, cor anglais and bass clarinet – plus a brass section which featured eight horns and no less than six harps. As for the strings, Wagner required 32 violins, 12 each of violas and cellos and 8 double basses. This characteristic extravagance of sound was created to provide greater delineation of tone colour, with each timbre represented, not merely as a voice but as a minature ensemble in itself, so that the true character of each instrumental colour is apparent even in the most complicated harmonies.

Instrument makers and instrumentalists also provided composers with the means for each and every flight of their creative imagination. The work of Theobald Boehm on the keywork (finger mechanism) of the flute and of Iwan Müller on the clarinet made it possible for performers to reach the new heights of dexterity and tonal subtlety that composers asked of them. Adolphe Sax and Auguste Mustel, both based in Paris, invented the saxophone and celeste respectively, while the French firm Erard made improvements in the harp.

One of the most important results of these orchestral innovations was the new role of the conductor. The orchestra itself had become an instrument to be 'played'. He alone was now responsible for the tonal balance, phrasing, tempo, flexibility and above all, for that element of personality that makes 'playing' into an interpretation. It is, therefore, very much to orchestral developments in this period that the conductor owes his star role today.

Wagner's contribution of more varied instruments and a wider spectrum of colour greatly extended the descriptive capacity of orchestral music of the late 19th century. The French especially, were greatly inspired by these possibilities. Composers such as Saint-Saëns, who introduced the symphonic poem to France: d'Indy, who promulgated Wagner's music: and Chausson, who was greatly influenced by it as well as by that of another Frenchman's – Massenet's similarly lush orchestration; all wrote vividly coloured descriptive pieces, though tempered by Gallic sophistication. In Germany, the Wagner legacy continued into the next century, culminating in the sometimes delicious, sometimes suffocating, but almost always overpowering orchestration of Richard Strauss, Mahler and Bruckner.

*Camille Saint-Saëns (left) was one of many French composers of the last century who wrote orchestral works of great beauty and subtlety.*

career, it is interesting to note that Rimsky is trying to avoid the influence of Wagner rather than waving a narrow national flag. To speak of and to the people was more important to him than trying to jam Russian dance tunes into a work. He is nonetheless aware of the danger and gives an interesting guide to the Capriccio: The opinion formed by both critics and the public, that the Capriccio is a 'magnificently orchestrated piece', is wrong. The Capriccio is a brilliant 'composition for orchestra'.

*The change of timbres, the felicitous choice of melodic designs and figuration patterns, exactly suiting each kind of instrument, brief virtuoso cadenzas for instruments, and so on, constitute here the very ESSENCE of composition and not its garb or orchestration. The Spanish themes, of dance character, furnished me with rich material for putting in use multiform orchestral effects. All in all, the Capriccio is undoubtedly a purely external piece, but vividly brilliant for all that.*

## *Programme notes*

The Capriccio is in five movements and is scored for piccolo, two flutes, two oboes, cor anglais, two clarinets, two bassoons, two trumpets, three trombones, four horns, bass tuba, side drums, kettle drums, bass drum, cymbals triangle, harp, strings, tambourine and castanets!

### I Alborada: Vivo e strepitoso

This alborada is a sort of instrumental explosion for full orchestra. An alborada is a 'dawn song', usually instrumental and, in Spain, often scored for folk oboe and drum. Rimsky's alborada would certainly rouse the listener in the early hours of the

*Rimsky-Korsakov's Capriccio Espagnol is a tour-de-force of instrumentation: true to the composer's main objective, it 'glitters with dazzling orchestral colour'. The individual character of the Spanish Dances (left) is expressed through a variety of musical means, including castanets! That this is very much a tourist's idea of Spain, however, is reflected in the delightful title page (far left).*

morning! The plucked strings give an impression of many guitars but are augmented by brass and drums. The movement ends with a violin solo.

## II Variazioni: Andante con moto

After the excitement of the opening, a horn announces a placid, graceful theme. There are five variations of this basic theme:

Example 3

These variations show a range not only of orchestral texture (cor anglais, pizzicato strings, solo flute) but also of emotional intensity from gentle calm to melancholy horn calls, a lyrical outcry on the upper strings and a dramatic response from the lower strings. An extended flute cadenza ends this movement.

## III Alborada: Vivo e strepitoso

This piece is the same melodic line as the first movement, but gives more fulsome display to the violins. Rimsky himself said:

*I was a little less successful in its third section where the brasses somewhat drown the melodic designs of the woodwinds; but this is very easy to remedy if the conductor will pay attention to it and moderate the indications of the shades of force in the brass instruments by replacing the fortissimo with a simple forte'.*

## IV Scena e Canto gitano: Allegretto

A drum roll and a trumpet fanfare open this piece. A solo violin restates the very Spanish sounding theme while the drums continue to sound very softly. Pizzicato strings lead to a flute solo, ornamented by cymbals and clarinets. A harp solo follows; then the tempo changes and the strings restate the complete theme of the gypsy song. Many different instruments are incorporated into the orchestral tapestry,

but the solo violin predominates.

## V Fandango asturiano: Allegretto

The fandango is a traditional Spanish dance of Andalusia performed by a couple; dancers tease and challenge each other exuberantly to mimic courtship rituals. Rimsky puts castanets and tambourines into the score as well as all the resources of his orchestra. Earlier themes are recalled and the Alborada theme is pounded out as a dramatic conclusion to the work.

Rimsky said that 'The Capriccio was to glitter with dazzling orchestral colour'. It was so successful that at rehearsals the orchestra applauded after the first movement – and every other part! Rimsky expressed his thanks by dedicating the piece to the orchestra of the Imperial Russian Opera House. Tchaikovsky who, although not one of the 'Mighty Handful', was friendly with most of them, wrote to Rimsky, 'Your *Capriccio Espagnol* is a colossal masterpiece of instrumentation and you may regard yourself as the greatest master of the present day'.

---

# Great interpreters

Polydor Ltd.

*The conductor, Daniel Barenboim (above)*

## Chicago Symphony Orchestra

Chicago's original orchestra performed from 1850 to 1868, under the conductor Julius Dyrhenfurth. It was named the Chicago Orchestra in 1891 but when its first conductor, Theodore Thomas, died in 1905, it was renamed the Theodore Thomas orchestra. It finally became the Chicago Symphony Orchestra in 1912.

The orchestra has had relatively few principal conductors, due mainly to the fact that Frederick Stock led them from 1905 until 1942. Since then, international fame has come with Fritz Reiner and his brilliant records and concert tours. He gave way to Jean Martino (1963–8), and then the present incumbent, Sir Georg Solti. Solti has kept the orchestra in the forefront of the recording world and enhanced its international reputation.

## Daniel Barenboim (conductor)

Of Russian descent, Barenboim was born in Argentina in 1942 and learned piano from his father. He gave his first recital when he was seven and, when his family moved to Europe, he played at the Salzburg Festival in 1952. He went on to study chamber music and conducting in Salzburg before the family finally settled in Israel. He studied in Paris under the legendary Nadia Boulanger and, in 1956, became the youngest person to receive the diploma of the Accademia di Santa Cecilia.

During the 1950's, Barenboim was known as an immensely gifted pianist and, in 1961, made his first appearance as a professional conductor. In 1964 he became a soloist with the English Chamber Orchestra and the following year conducted a Mozart Piano Concerto from the keyboard with them. This was the start of a long association with the ECO, both in

concert and in the studio.

Throughout the 1960's, Barenboim continued to perform as a soloist. He also won much praise for his recording of the Beethoven Piano Sonatas and, in 1968, made his conducting debut with the London Symphony Orchestra in New York. Since then he has conducted many top orchestras, including the Chicago Symphony Orchestra.

In 1967 he married the British cellist Jacqueline du Pré and together they gave many concerts, as well as making superb recordings of such works as Elgar's Cello Concerto before illness tragically cut short her career. Still a relatively young man, Barenboim has a wealth of experience behind him and still pursues both pianistic and conducting careers. He has made superb solo and outstanding lieder records, including those with the great baritone, Dietrich Fischer-Dieskau.

---

## FURTHER LISTENING

**Borodin**
1 Symphony no. 2 in B Minor (1876)
2 String Quartet no. 2 in D (1885)
3 String Quartet no. 1 in A (1874-9)

**Mussorgsky**
1 Pictures at an Exhibition (piano version)
2 Pictures at an Exhibition (orchestrated by Ravel)
3 The Nursery – Song cycle (1872)
4 Boris Godunov – Opera (1874) (version by Rimsky-Korsakov)

**Balakirev**
1 Symphony no. 1 in C (1866-89)
2 Islamey – Oriental Fantasy (1869)

**Taneyev**
1 Symphony no. 1 in C Minor, op. 12
2 Piano Trio in D, op. 22

**Anton Rubinstein**
1 Piano Sonata no. 3, op. 41
2 The Demon – Opera (1875)

**Glazunov**
1 Violin Concerto in A Minor, op. 82
2 Concerto for Saxophone & Strings
3 The Seasons, op. 67 – Ballet

**Scriabin**
1 Poème de l'Extase, op. 54
2 Prometheus – Poem of Fire, op. 60
3 Piano Sonata no. 2 in G Minor, op. 19

# IN THE BACKGROUND
# *'Conquer or perish'*

*Russia's defeat in the Crimean War resulted in her loss of world standing, but it heralded reforms which were to transform Russian society and inspire the great nationalist composers.*

*Russia's expansionist ambitions were considered a threat to the European balance of power — an intolerable situation for Britain and France who had much to lose, namely sea power and routes to India and the Near East. Events escalated into full-scale war, starting in 1854, and the conflict gave rise to a series of bloody battles (left).*

*Catherine the Great's dream of restoring the Christian Byzantine Empire provided her grandson, Nicholas I, with the good excuse to intervene in the internal affairs of the Ottoman (Turkish) Empire and thus gain a valuable means of improving Russia's position in areas under Turkish control. Jerusalem (above) was just one of the cities in Turkish-ruled Palestine and when Russia demanded Orthodox rights over the Holy Places in the city, both Britain and France were prompted to try and protect what they saw as their common spiritual homeland. This was the cue for British and French involvement.*

The Crimean War (1854-56) was the first large-scale war between the great powers after 40 years of relative peace. The War, which arose out of the Russian Tsar Nicholas I's expansionist ambitions in the Turkish Empire was, in many respects, fumbling, futile and costly both financially and in human lives. Russia's eventual humiliating defeat, however, was instructive in showing up the backwardness of Russian society (and also the army) and the defects of autocratic rule. As such it was instrumental in paving the way for reforms, the most important being the emancipation of the serfs.

### The zealous Tsar: Nicholas I

When Nicholas I came to the throne in 1825, succeeding his brother Alexander I, he became ruler of a country strangled by excessive bureaucracy and hampered by a corrupt legal system, and only the bare rudiments of public education. Russian agriculture was highly inefficient, with the work on the farms carried out by serfs (peasant slaves) using antiquated methods. Russian industry was still in its infancy compared with that in western Europe, with the result that its low level of productivity of coal and iron retarded the growth of other heavy industry and a more industrialised society.

During his reign Alexander I had instituted some administrative and legal reforms, broadened the educational base and made tentative steps towards mitigating the worst effects of serfdom. Alexander's reforming impetus, however, was curbed by conservative opinion and as a result Alexander turned his back on the liberal principle with which he had some sympathy. A period of reaction set in.

This continued under Nicholas. He had been alarmed first by the Decembrists' attempted coup in 1825, then by the revolutions sweeping through Europe in 1830-31, convulsing France, Belgium,

German and Italian states and, closer to home, Poland. Now, turning his back on all progressive influences, he abolished Alexander's liberal university statutes, and confined higher education to the upper classes whom he saw as less politically dangerous. At the same time he banned public meetings and foreign travel, and in a move that verged on the psychotic, he had music scores and the dots in books scrutinised for secret cyphers. Books were savagely censored, and those which contravened acceptable ideas were expunged.

In 1826 he created the Third Section and Corps of Gendarmes, the political police which had spies and informers in libraries, schools and even private homes. Those voicing ideologically unacceptable ideas ran the gravest risks, with intellectual deviants being exiled or incarcerated in lunatic asylums. Said Nicholas of himself, 'I am a sentry at the outpost to see all and observe all.' To which his critics (including the Zapadniki, who looked to Europe for Russia's origins and destiny and saw their country remade in the image of western science, free thought, liberty, rationalism and individualism) would add 'and to stifle all independent thought.'

In his endeavours Nicholas was supported by the Slavophiles, whose slogan was 'Autocracy, Orthodoxy and Nationalism'. The Slavophiles believed that the true future of Russia was based in the peasant commune and in Orthodox Christianity and they were, in their way, precursors of the Nationalist composers in digging down to the roots of Russian history and traditions. Indeed as his reign proceeded Nicholas took ever more seriously his God-given right to rule, and he became convinced of his infallibility and divine mission.

When revolutions again fired Europe in 1848, Nicholas expanded his role to that of a vigilante. He closed Russia's frontiers to prevent the spread of

*The Bridgeman Art Library*

*Tsar Nicholas I (left), a vigorous and cruel despot, was not content to confine his power to his own country. He wished to see Russia's frontiers extended in every direction, and it was to prevent him taking control of the Balkans and Constantinople that the Crimean War was fought.*

grandmother, Empress Catherine II (the Great: 1729–96), had already made significant gains – Ottoman Turkey. Catherine's achievements fell short of her ultimate ambition to restore the long-gone Christian Byzantine Empire. Nevertheless her activities, which included the annexation of the Crimea in 1783, and those of subsequent rulers, including Nicholas I, had squeezed from the Sultan important navigating, territorial and protectorate rights and also a decided influence on the welfare of Turkey's Orthodox Christians.

Nicholas' attempt in 1833 to gain a free hand in the Dardanelles by means of cynical diplomacy was thwarted in 1841 by Britain and France, who had long been involved with the 'Eastern Question' – a problem posed since the start of the 19th century by the growing weakness of Turkey. They were especially alarmed by Nicholas' constant reference to Turkey as a 'Sick Man' stricken with a terminal disease, whose effects should be parcelled out among the major European powers. The straits Convention of 1841 obliged Russia, together with the other signatories – Britain, France, Austria, Prussia and Turkey – to ban all foreign warships from entering the Dardanelles and Bosphorus in times of peace. This outlawed any exclusive foreign influence over the sea, the very advantage Nicholas sought.

### Run-up to the Crimean War

Undaunted, Nicholas raised an issue justifiably linked with Russian interests in Turkey – Orthodox Christianity.

In January 1853 Nicholas demanded Orthodox rights in the holy places in Turkish-ruled Palestine – and also acknowledgement from the Sultan that Russia was protector of all his twelve million Christian Slav subjects. On the advice of the British ambassador, the Sultan agreed to the first demand but not to the second, which would have given the Tsar too much power within the Turkish Empire.

The religious cast which Nicholas gave to his attempt at challenging Turkish sovereignty fooled no one. The Austrian Minister in Paris observed that the Tsar was viewed in France as a tyrant 'ready to cover his plans of conquest and invasion with the mantle of religion'. Although Britain was concerned on a wider front by a crisis that could upset the balance of power in the Near East and spread ripples through British interests in Persia, Egypt and as far as India, the French were more directly involved. The new French emperor, Napoleon III, personally detested Nicholas and longed to prove himself the heir of Bonaparte and avenge Bonaparte's defeat in Russia in 1812. In addition, in Palestine, Russia's proteges, the Orthodox monks and Napoleon's, the Catholic monks, were in dispute over possession of the door keys to the Church of the Nativity in Bethlehem and the arrangements for the upkeep of the holy places; also, the Catholics claimed the Orthodox had stolen the silver star from the Grotto of the Nativity.

Magnified and exploited by the ambitions of Nicholas and Napoleon III, this squabble rapidly grew into a *cause célèbre* after the Tsar made monumental errors of judgement. First he failed to credit that Napoleon would actively pursue the Catholic cause in the holy places. Next he failed to realize that his anti-liberal campaigns had made him hated in Britain and that neither the British government nor the press could stand by while he bullied the Sultan and asserted Russian rights over those of the French.

revolutionary ideas; sent troops to help the Austrian Emperor quell rebellion in Hungary; and threatened to send a further army if the German revolutionaries declared a republic. The monarchies of Europe survived 1848, and Nicholas came out of it as a saviour, the 'mighty potentate' as Queen Victoria called him. However to the French minister at St Petersburg, Nicholas appeared as 'this great spoiled child', and one seeking fresh fields in which to display his glory.

### Nicholas' expansionist ambitions

Nicholas was not content with dictating his will at home; he wished to extend his influences abroad. To this end he turned to the sphere where his

*This contemporary British Cartoon (left), entitled 'The Imperial Eagle imprisons the Turkey', sums up the British feeling of the time towards Russia's bullying of weakling Turkey.*

*Michael Holford*

*Despite the fact that the war was going badly for them, and that the French and British had successfully bombarded Odessa (right), the Russians steadfastly refused to pay the price of peace – an end to their interference in Turkey's dominions.*

Given these miscalculations, Nicholas felt free to threaten the Sultan in May 1853: the Tsar's demand must be met within eight days or Russian forces would occupy Turkish Moldavia and Wallachia to force the issue. In response British and French naval squadrons were ordered into Turkish waters, but Nicholas was undeterred and a Russian army, 8,000 strong, duly occupied the Turkish provinces.

A furious round of diplomacy ensued. Peace plans were fielded. The Turks demonstrated angrily. Press and public in Britain and France came out fiercely against Russia. Then, on 27 September 1853, the Turkish Sultan, snug in the military protection of Britain and France, threatened war if the Russian troops were not withdrawn within eighteen days. Nicholas responded with a manifesto informing his people that they were being forced to fight to protect 'the sacred rights of the Orthodox Church'.

The Russians responded patriotically, and Slavophiles hailed the imminent conflict as a promise of liberation for Slavs from the infidel Turks, and from the Austrians. A leading Slavophile, the poet Fedor Dyutchev wrote exultantly:

*And beneath the ancient vault of St Sophia
(Constantinople) in reborn
Byzantium will stand once more Christ's altar.
Kneel down before it, O Tsar of Russia, and arise
Tsar of all the Slavs.*

*Balaclava harbour in 1855 (above). It was here that the British built the first military railroad to carry men and supplies to the front line.*

By contrast the expatriate Zapadniki Alexander Herzen acidly remarked that the Russian officialdom then lumbering into combat was 'a dumb unit without a flag and without a name, the cord of slavery round its neck . . . with the insolent pretensions of the Byzantine Empire.'

### War is declared

Turkey declared war on Russia on 4 October 1853. The Sultan's forces crossed the Danube and took up a position at Kalafat, where they endangered the right flank of the Russian invaders. The Turks fortified Kalafat and other positions on the north bank of the Danube and awaited the Russian countermoves. In Constantinople, British, French, Austrian and Prussian representatives urged the Sublime Porte, the Turkish government, to hold back hostilities. Hostilities nevertheless commenced after the Russians declared war on the Turks (1 November). There were skirmishes at Kalafat and then, on 2 November, the Russians attacked the 3,000 Turks dug in at Oltenitza. Though outnumbered three to one, the Turks repulsed the onslaught. Two further Russian attacks on 3 and 4 November likewise failed.

After some early successes, the Russians were in

*'A Russian Convoy on the Halt' (left). This drawing appeared in the* Illustrated Times *(a contemporary periodical) of 11 August 1855, which described the long and wearisome journey of the ill-equipped Russian soldiers across the steppes of the Crimea.*

*Shortly after war was declared with Russia, the famous English nurse, Florence Nightingale, arrived at Scutari, near Constantinople, to set up a nursing department (right). She gained a heroic reputation for tending the wounded.*

similar difficulties against the Turks on the Black Sea coast. In October 1853, the Turks captured Fort St Nicholas near Batum, and held it despite repeated Russian attempts to retrieve it.

By the end of November, however, the balance of triumph was redressed in Russia's favour. On 30 November a Russian fleet surprised a poorly armed Turkish force sheltering in harbour at Sinope on the north coast of Asia Minor. In the first demonstration of the devastating power of their navy, the Russians sent a waterfall of shells smashing into the Turks. The slaughter and destruction were appalling and the Russians showed no mercy. The Turkish squadron was left a mass of broken, burning timbers. Some 5,000 sailors died and the survivors were blasted in the water by Russian grapeshot.

Sinope was widely regarded as an atrocity, and hardened Anglo-French attitudes to Russia. The British and French fleets entered the Black Sea on 3rd January 1854, and on 27th February, a joint ultimatum was sent to Nicholas; unless Russian troops withdrew from Moldavia and Wallachia by the end of April, declaration of war would follow. It came sooner. The Tsar made no reply and the British and French proclaimed war on 28 March.

Tsar Nicholas had blundered into a conflict which was to kill half a million Russians — some in battle, most from cholera and other diseases. Men and material had to be sent overland to the Crimea at fearful cost, and on the three month trek overland to the front, many Russian soldiers died. Aside from their own raw courage, and the fact that circumstances were also grim for their opponents, the ordinary Russian soldier — generally a serf — had little that was needed to fight a modern war: poor armament, meagre or non-existent medical facilities, tainted water, mouldy meat, biscuits alive with weevils, rotten boots, inadequate clothing. Equally, the bulk of the Russian Navy was out of date.

The war went badly for Russia from the start. Pressure from an Anglo-French expeditionary force, landed at Varna on the Black Sea, and an Austrian army, 5000 strong, which moved into Moldavia and Wallachia, forced the Russians to evacuate the Balkans by early August. In addition, French and British ships bombarding Odessa caused serious damage to the Russian shore batteries. On 8 August, the Allies offered peace conditions, which included an end to Russian interference in Turkey. The Russians refused.

The Allies now turned to a plan to break Russian naval power in the Black Sea by crippling the naval base at Sevastopol. Here, by the end of summer 1854, most of the Russian fleet was blocked in and Allied warships had also sealed off other Russian ports and the mouths of the Danube.

In the eastern Black Sea, British and Turkish naval squadrons captured or destroyed several Russian forts and on land, the Sultan's ally, the legendary Daghestan chieftain Shamyl, suddenly appeared before Kars (now Northeast Turkey) with 20,000 men and the Russian garrison had to retreat in such haste that they burned what they could not carry.

On 14 September, Prince Menshikov, Russian commander in the Crimea, with 80,000 men at his disposal, allowed 57,000 Allied troops, transported in warships from Varna, to land unopposed at Evpatoria. From there they moved south against Sevastopol. Six days later, Menchikov's army made a stand on the heights above the River Alma but failed, despite a naturally defensible position, to bar the Allies' path to the naval base. Over 5700 Russians died.

### The siege of Sevastopol

The squeeze on Sevastopol began in earnest on 17 October, with a punishing Allied artillery bombardment. The Russian engineer, Colonel Eduard Todleben had constructed a mighty network of defences, heavily laced with artillery posts, and while fire and counterfire caused heavy casualties, the defences were barely damaged. Sevastopol now settled down to a siege which was to last 349 days.

A week later, Menshikov attempted to drive a wedge between the siege lines and the British base at the Black Sea supply port of Balaklava, six miles southeast of Sevastopol. The ensuing battle, on 25 October 1854, is chiefly know for the Charge of the Light Brigade (later immortalized by Lord Tennyson in a poem). This monument to great heroism and tactical mismanagement by British military leaders prompted the remark by the French General Pierre Bosquet: 'C'est magnifique mais ce n'est pas la guerre.'

Strategically more significant, however, was the Russians' failure to fight through the British defences. The huge mass of Russian cavalry was sent off by the 'thin red line' of the 500 men of the 93rd Highlanders, whose long-range fire made them wheel off left after two volleys, wheel again after the third and then retreat. Just as ignominious was the way 900 cavalry of the British Heavy Brigade, fighting hand to hand, hacked about so effectively among 3,000 Russians that the latter faltered and melted away.

In his next attempt at breakthrough at Inkerman on 5 November, Menshikov sought to surprise the British by attacking at two in the morning over country thick with oak scrub and obscured by fog. The British, however, responded with alacrity and there followed a series of small but savagely contested actions in which the Russians, committed piecemeal to the battle, were gradually over-whelmed by their opponents, who were reinforced in strength as the hours went by. The battle was, nevertheless, finely balanced until 9.30 a.m. when two British 18-pounder guns were dragged to

*On the heights above the River Alma, Franco-British forces, with Turkish support, attacked Prince Menshikov's troops (below) forcing them to beat a hasty retreat to Sevastopol – an opening move in what was to become one of the major centres of conflict in the war.*

Inkerman by 150 men, and half an hour later the French General Bosquet arrived with 2,000 fresh infantry. By noon the Russians were in retreat, having suffered grievous losses: 10,729 men out of an original 42,000. British and French losses were likewise punishing – 3516 killed and wounded – and their victory had been hollow: now they would be unable to capture Sevastopol before that remorseless ally of the Russians, the winter, began.

### Disillusion and death

As the winter of 1854-55 froze in, the famous reports sent back by William Howard Russell of *The Times* were paralleled in Russia by the despatches of Count Leo Tolstoy. Like Russell's, Tolstoy's news was full of the fortitude and suffering of the ordinary soldier, and he succeeded in badly ruffling the confidence of both Tsar Nicholas and his more educated subjects. Nicholas was personally shattered by the shape the war had taken, and the fact that it was a Pandora's box, revealing the crucial ineffectiveness of a once much vaunted army and of the bureaucracy.

Nicholas himself confided a desperate resolve in a letter to King Frederick William IV of Prussia: 'Nothing remains for me now but to fight, but to conquer or perish, with honour, like a martyr of our holy faith.' This letter was written in the summer of 1854, before the disastrous inadequacies of the Russian army had been fully revealed. By the winter of 1854-55, Nicholas caught a chill which turned into pneumonia. He died at the Winter Palace on 2 March – without the honour he had sought.

### Sevastopol continues

By the time Nicholas died, the Allied position in the Crimea was much strengthened. Seventeen thousand Sardinian reinforcements had arrived at Balaclava. The British constructed a rail link between Balaclava and the lines: by the end of April, it was handling 240 tons of stores and ammunition daily. A half-hearted Russian attempt at interference at Evpatoria on 17 February was repulsed by the Turks, and from then on the Russian position weakened.

*Museo del Risorgimento, Rome/AISA*

*BBC Hulton Picture Library*

*When Russian garrisons lost their strongholds at Malakov (above) and at Redan, the troops under siege at Sevastopol knew that they could hold out no longer, and that they were on the point of losing the war.*

*Tsar Nicholas' error of judgement was to cost the lives of half a million Russians – the harsh conditions claiming as many victims as the battles themselves. The long trek overland to the front was morale-sapping and tough – and hampered by roads clogged with mud, sometimes frozen over with snow and littered with horses which had perished from hunger and thirst (left).*

Bombardment of Sevastopol by 138 British and 362 French guns (8-18 April) destroyed most of Todleben's splendid defences, and some 6000 Russians were killed.

On 24 May the Allies captured Kerch at the entrance to the Sea of Azov, so severing Russian communications with the interior and opening the waterway to Allied gunboats to attack Russian coastal shipping. On 7 June Sevastopol came under bombardment yet again, and the Russians lost 8500 men while failing to prevent Allied troops seizing the outer works. At Malakov and the Redan on 17 and 18 June, the defenders managed to throw back enemy attacks, especially at the Redan where the British were decimated by crossfire from 100 Russian guns.

The siege was now sapping Russian strength at Sevastopol at the rate of 350 men per day during July 1855 alone. On 16 August, in a final effort to halt the slide, the Russians tried again to break through the siege lines. Five hours of ferocious combat ended in more failure: 3229 Russians were killed and 5000 wounded. The last chance to relieve Sevastopol had gone and the end came on 8 September 1855, after a meticulously planned and executed operation by General Bosquet's corps which swept the Russian garrisons from the strongpoints at Malakov and the Redan. That night the Russians blew up the remaining fortifications in Sevastopol and evacuated the fortress.

Elsewhere, the war was going badly for Russia. On 16 October three French ironclads blasted to pieces vital Russian forts at the mouth of the River Bug, Russian counter fire proving utterly ineffective. On 21 November, Sweden joined the alliance against Russia. Then, on 29 December, Austria, until then neutral, threatened war unless Russia made peace and accepted the cession of Bessarabia and the neutrality of the Black Sea.

## The aftermath

The peace treaty was signed in Paris in March 1856. Under its terms Russia had to yield part of the province of Bessarabia to the Turks; the navy was no longer to use the Black Sea as a warship base; captured Turkish cities were to be yielded up and an undertaking given that Russia would never interfere in Turkey again. The new Tsar, Nicholas' son Alexander II, found the peace terms inexpressibly bitter, and was chastened by Russia's humiliating defeat and its loss in world standing.

Nevertheless some good came out of the disaster of the war which pointed out so clearly the reactionary nature of Russia. In 1861 Alexander emancipated the serfs, and he followed this with penal reform, the creation of *zemtsvo,* a new unit of local government, encouragement of secondary education and university reform, and changes in army and navy administration. Culture also took a step forward. The St. Petersburg Conservatory of Music was founded (1862) and here Tchaikovsky was an early student. After 1871 Rimsky-Korsakov was Professor of Composition and Instrumentation. The Free School of Music, which opened in rivalry to the Conservatory, had Mily Balakirev as its prinicipal concert conductor and the example of St. Petersburg was soon followed by a Moscow Conservatory.

Tragically, however, the hope for the future this might have fostered was overshadowed by the cardinal weakness bred into Alexander. As a result it was as a tyrant that Alexander II was eventually assassinated in 1881. Yet only a few hours earlier 'the Liberator' had been at work on plans for a limited form of national representative government. After his murder his son, Tsar Alexander III, who was unambiguously cast in the autocratic mould, found the plan manifesto unsigned on his father's desk. Without hesitation he tore it up and threw it away.

*After two long hard years, the Crimean War – started as a result of diplomatic blunders – came to an end. The peace treaty was signed in Paris in March 1856 (right), with the humiliated Russians promising never again to interfere in Turkey.*

Réunion des musées nationaux

# THE GREAT COMPOSERS

# *Nikolay Rimsky-Korsakov*

## *(1844–1908)*

*Nikolay Rimsky-Korsakov was the most productive member of the 'Mighty Handful' of Russian nationalist composers. His works are rich in colour and texture, enhanced by his unique understanding of orchestration. He also helped to establish Russian music as an editor, especially of Mussorgsky's work, and as a teacher; his students included Prokofiev and Stravinsky. Although he professed to know nothing about music theory when he began teaching, he became one of the world's greatest music theorists. Many of his works were based upon Russian history and folklore. With Scheherazade, however, analysed in the* Listener's Guide, *Rimsky-Korsakov sought to express a colourful, oriental flavour. Europeans had long been fascinated with the East; the tales of the Arabian Nights, which Scheherazade was based on, contained all the elements of oriental exotica that so entranced Europeans, as* In The Background *describes.*

*Nikolay Rimsky-Korsakov was born in the small town of Tikhvin in 1844; his rural upbringing gave him early exposure to the folk songs of Russia. He continued to study music upon entering naval cadet school in 1856; in 1861, he was introduced to Balakirev, who collaborated with him on a symphony. Tours of duty in England, America and the Mediterranean divided his attention, but upon his return to St. Petersburg in 1865, Rimsky met Borodin and premièred his Symphony in E flat minor. He took the post of professor of composition at the St. Petersburg Conservatoire, at the same time composing copiously under the nationalist aims of the 'Mighty Handful'. His interest in the folk songs he had known as a child inspired richly melodic operas and symphonies. During the last few years of his life, political events in Russia upset him deeply; his work was supressed and he was forced to resign his post. He died in 1908.*

**COMPOSER'S LIFE**

# 'My musical life'

*In turning from a naval career to his real love, music, Rimsky-Korsakov produced a number of stunning compositions, as well as orchestrating many works for great contemporary composers.*

*(Above) Sophia Vasilyevna and Andrey Petrovich Rimsky-Korsakov – Nikolay Rimsky-Korsakov's parents.*

Rimsky-Korsakov, seen by his friends as an even-tempered and precise man, led a life largely determined by his art – and his art took a winding, at times, treacherous, path. But his intense energy carried him through the epoch of Russian nationalism in music into the 20th century and modernism. Of the Mighty Handful – Balakirev, Mussorgsky, Rimsky-Korsakov, Borodin and Cui – Rimsky-Korsakov was the most productive.

Nikolay Andreyevich Rimsky-Korsakov was born on 18 March 1844 in the small town of Tikhvin where his 60-year-old father had been living in retirement with his second wife. He was their second son; Voin – their eldest – was 22 when Nikolay was born.

It was a highly musical home. His father could thump out a few bars from operas on their old piano, but it was his mother who was the strongest influence – and the earliest one. 'Before I was two', he noted in his memoirs, 'I could distinguish all the melodies my mother sang me; at three or four I was an expert at beating time on a drum to my father's piano playing . . .then I began to pick out the pieces with the harmonies myself on the piano; and having learned the names of the notes, would stand in another room and call them out when they were struck.' Although from the age of six he had piano lessons from various people – neighbours and acquaintances. musical life in Tikhvin was limiting.

### The call of the sea
Apart from a visit to his uncle, Admiral Nicholas, in St. Petersburg, by the time he was 12 he had only left Tikhvin three times – to visit friends in the country. As a child his driving ambition was to be a sailor, just like his elder brother, Voin, to whom he was devoted. In July 1856 Rimsky aged 12 went to St. Petersburg to enter the Corps of Naval Cadets, where he proved himself a good cadet.

At the Cadet School he took music lessons from an indifferent teacher and as a result made little progress. However, weekends spent with family friends – the Golovins – introduced him to Italian opera. Symphony concerts in 1859-60 given at the Grand Theatre aroused his interest in Beethoven and Mendelssohn, so much so that he spent all his pocket money on buying tickets and scores. Glinka, who had died in 1857, became his hero and he set about orchestrating the entr'actes in Glinka's *A Life for the Tsar* with little or no knowledge of the instruments.

In 1857 his brother Voin became commander of the gunnery instruction ship *Prokbor,* and for

two summers Rimsky spent time on board under his brother's supervision. Back at the Cadet School, in 1859, he acquired a better music teacher – Canille – who shared his pupil's admiration of Glinka, considering him 'a great genius' and *Ruslan* 'the best opera in the world'.

Significantly it was Canille who, on 8 December 1861, introduced Rimsky to one of the Mighty Handful – M. A. Balakirev. Balakirev's personality and drive worked miracles on the youth who was tempted to show Balakirev some 'watery' piano pieces he

*While a student at the Naval Cadet School, Rimsky continued his musical studies with Théodore Canille. Through him he met Balakirev (above) one of the influential composers known as 'The Mighty Handful'. Balakirev took Rimsky under his wing, and although over the years their friendship soured, it was Balakirev who influenced Rimsky to turn to music for a career.*

*Rimsky was devoted to his brother Voin, 22 years his senior, and although he had a musical upbringing set his heart on joining Voin in a naval career. After passing out from Naval Cadet School in April 1862 he set sail as a midshipman (above: front row, left).*

had written, a scherzo in C minor and his Symphony in E flat minor. Through Canille he also met Cui and Mussorgsky. Rimsky was totally absorbed by the musical shop talk, and although years later he would blame Balakirev for narrowing his musical tastes, at this point Balakirev collaborated with Rimsky on his symphony. The young composer's flair for instrumentation revealed itself as the work progressed but the symphony was the casualty of constant interruption. Rimsky-Korsakov left Naval College in 1862 as *gardemarine* and was assigned to the clipper *Almaz* for a two-year cruise. Rimsky-Korsakov was desperate at the thought of leaving his recently discovered musical friends, but his brother was adamant that he continue his naval career and so on 2 November he set sail.

England was the first stop – nearly four months at Gravesend for re-rigging. In London he did a little sight-seeing and settled into a leisurely life on board ship – reading and discussing politics with other officers. Music was not entirely abandoned – in response to Balakirev's letters urging him to continue with the slow movement of his symphony, he worked at it and completed it. Since there was no piano on board, the locals at a Gravesend pub had the honour of hearing Rimsky-Korsakov play through the movement.

From England the *Almaz* sailed to the Baltic to put a stop to the practice of gun-running to Polish rebels – a group Rimsky-Korsakov and other officers secretly agreed with – before returning to Kronstadt for a few days. Then in 1863 when it looked as though war with England was certain, the *Almaz* was despatched to New York to intercept merchant ships. The war never happened. So while the squadron wallowed in

F. X. Winterhalter 'Madame Rimsky-Korsakov'. Compiegne-Chateau. Lauros-Giraudon

*In the spring of 1868 Rimsky met the Purgold sisters at musical evenings given by his composer friend, Dargomizhky. Soon he was friends with the whole Purgold family and in December 1871 was engaged to Nadhezhda Purgold (above). They were married on 12 July 1872 at First Pargolovo, the summer home of the Purgold's, with Mussorgsky as best man. Immediately after the wedding supper the couple went to the Warsaw Station in St Petersburg to embark on an extensive honeymoon in Switzerland and Italy. In his autobiography Rimsky outlines their travels, including a visit to Rigi (left).*

Albert Goodwin 'Righi'. Townley Hall Art Gallery, Burnley. Bridgeman Art Library

peaceful waters Rimsky-Korsakov took excursions to the Chesapeake Falls, Washington, Niagara and, in the tradition of the service, there was no lack of wine, women and song.

Finally, after an exotic Mediterranean tour the squadron returned to Kronstadt in 1865. When he arrived back in St. Petersburg, Rimsky saw clearly that he 'became an officer-dilettante, who sometimes enjoyed playing or listening to music; but all my dreams of artistic activity had completely flown away. Nor did I regret them.' However when he resumed his friendship with Balakirev whose Free School of Music was gaining momentum, his musical appetite was once again stirred. There was a new member of the group – A. P. Borodin, a professor of chemistry experimenting with his first symphony. Rimsky's E flat minor Symphony, completed under Balakirev's supervision, received its premiere at the Free School – Rimsky, looking youthful and serious in his naval uniform, took the considerable applause.

Shortly after this modest triumph, Rimsky was introduced to the sister of Glinka, Lyudmila Shastakova at whose house he was to become a regular visitor. His naval duties took up only a few hours each day – and so with his symphony behind him compositions began to flow more easily. A bundle of melodies brought back from a visit to the Caucasus by Balakirev awakened in Rimsky an interest in Oriental music.

In June 1866, at his brother's villa at Tervayoki, near Vyborg, Rimsky began work on *Sadko*, a 'musical picture' about the legend of a Novgorod merchant suggested by Mussorgsky. In the summer of 1868 Rimsky and Mussorgsky became firm friends – and in the autumn they moved in to a single room together where they lived and worked on their operas *The Maid of Pskov* and *Boris Godunov*, respectively.

Earlier in 1868 the composer Dargomīzhsky provided his musical friends with a new weekly rendezvous at his house – it was here that Rimsky met the sisters Alexandra and Nadezhda Purgold. Nadezhda, an elegant pianist, then aged 20 became his wife a few years later.

### New directions

Azanchevsky, the new Director of St. Petersburg Conservatoire, offered Rimsky the Professorship of practical composition and instrumentation plus the direction of the orchestral class – all areas that had suffered under the previous Director. Azanchevsky knew that Rimsky was an amateur, but he thought his enthusiasm would give the department new impetus. Not only was Rimsky an amateur, however, but he was technically ignorant.

*'It was not merely that I couldn't at that time have harmonized a chorale properly, had never written a single contrapuntal exercise in my life . . . but I didn't even know the names of . . . the chords . . . As for conducting, I had never conducted an orchestra in my life . . .'*

His ignorance went undetected, mainly because of the energy with which Rimsky went about studying to keep up with his own students. Needless to say, he went on to become one of the best teachers of composition Russia has had.

Voin, who had gone to Italy for a rest cure, died at Pisa in November 1871 and Rimsky was despatched to bring home his body. A surprise consequence of this tragedy was that Rimsky became the favourite of Krabbe, the Minister of Marine. Krabbe's influence even extended as far as the official censor and he was able to smooth out some little difficulties Rimsky was having with his *Maid of Pskov*, then under scrutiny.

A month after Voin's death Rimsky became engaged to Nadezhda Purgold and, in the summer of 1872 Rimsky and Nadezhda married, with Mussorgsky as best man. The honeymoon trip took in Switzerland, the Italian lakes, Vienna and Warsaw.

In January 1873 Krabbe created a new post with a good salary especially for Rimsky – Inspector of Naval Bands. Rimsky took his duties seriously and although he knew little about naval band techniques he taught himself the basics so that soon any criticism from him was taken as authoritative. Later that year the first of his six children – Michael ('Misha') – was born.

Balakirev, in 1874, was still acting Director of the flagging Free School of Music, but the committee members persuaded him to resign and hand over to Rimsky; Mussorgsky interpreted this as an act of treachery and as he became more remote to Rimsky, so Rimsky drew closer to the Borodins.

That summer he took his wife and son to Nikolaev on the Black Sea to inspect the band of the naval garrison. From there they travelled to Sevastopol to the south of Crimea. In one of the towns, Bakhchisaray, Rimsky heard genuine Eastern music for the first time from the teeming street musicians.

On his return to St Petersburg he started on his programme of revitalizing the Free School. For their first concert since 1872, when Balakirev had retired, what should Rimsky, the erstwhile modernist, choose to put on but a concert in which the latest composer was Haydn! It seemed as though Mussorgsky was right and all but Borodin gave him up as a lost cause. Rimsky steeped himself in technique and, while Nadezhda slowly recovered from a serious illness brought on by the birth of their second child, Sonya, Rimsky produced dry and uninspired piano pieces. The first of the Free School concerts in 1876 was nearly all Bach and Handel, but he redeemed himself in the eyes of his colleagues by putting on a second that was all Russian.

Fortunately two things gave him new direction. He began studying folk songs and he took on the editing of Glinka's scores. Collaborating with Fillipov in 1877 he completed his *Collection of One Hundred Russian Folk Songs*, and in doing so regained the respect of Mussorgsky. That same year he began his fascinating, if not totally reliable, *Record of my*

*The colourful set design (above) captures the exotic nature of the music of Rimsky-Korsakov's later operas based on a Pushkin tale entitled* **The Fairy tale of Tsar Saltan.** *The full title of Rimsky's opera gives further clues to its fantastic nature:* **The Tale of Tsar Saltan, of his son the famous and mighty hero Prince Gvidon Saltanovich and of the beautiful Swan Princess!** *The opera was completed at the beginning of 1900 and received its first performance in Moscow in November 1900.*

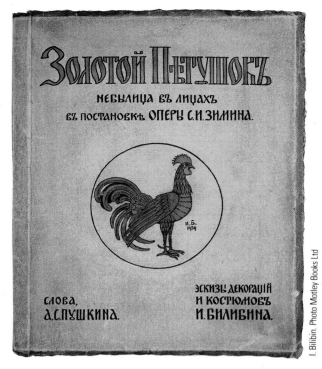

*In October 1906, on his return from a family holiday at Riva on Lake Garda, Rimsky began work on what was to be his last opera,* **The Golden Cockerel.** *It was first performed a year after his death in 1909 by the Zimin Opera Company at the Solodnikov Theatre in Moscow. The cover of the souvenir programme for that performance is shown right.*

*Musical Life,* which he then laid aside for 12 years. There was little time for relaxation: apart from his official duties and his private pupils – he had the Free School concerts to prepare.

The Free School was always in financial difficulties and like any amateur organization it contained musicians who were bad to indifferent. So it was with some relief that Rimsky handed back to Balakirev its Direction in September 1881, admitting that he was 'a thousand times more suited to the position than I.'

He interrupted his summer holiday in 1882 with a visit to Moscow for the All-Russian Art and Industrial Exhibition where he was invited to conduct a couple of concerts. He included in one of his programmes the First Symphony of one of his most gifted students – the 16-year-old Sasha Glazunov. It was on this occasion that he met the wealthy music lover, Belyayev.

With the accession of Alexander III came many changes, including the end of Bakhmetev's long reign as Intendant of the Imperial Chapel. The influential Fillipov was active as ever and saw to it

*One of the original costume designs for the first performance of* **The Golden Cockerel** *(right). Rimsky found that although he was not able to work on the score uninterruptedly the composition went well and it was completed in 1907. However, the same could not be said for the libretto by Bel'sky, based on a tale by Pushkin about the stupidity of the aristocracy. This met with hostility from the official censor and permission for it to be published or performed was withheld unless 45 lines were cut – no doubt problems of this nature made the last months of the already ill Rimsky-Korsakov more difficult.*

Они уволили...

present year has been very unlucky for me; I've had nothing but dangers and commotion, and all this has descended on my unfortunate *Mlada,* which will probably be my last composition . . . (at any rate, the last important one)'.

The unlucky streak continued: the 25th anniversary of his becoming a composer was marred by a silly row with Balakirev, and at home the baby, Slavchik, died and Masha, the second youngest child, fell ill soon afterwards. Thinking the air would do Masha some good they spent the summer of 1891 in Switzerland. The air made little difference to Masha, and Rimsky found he could not work and tore up the book he was writing in a fit of bitterness.

By the summer of 1892 he was in the thick of a real mental and physical crisis. He devoured anything written on philosophy and aesthetics in a manic search for an answer to some vague question about himself. With no appetite for music he spent his time 'thinking and thinking and making notes . . .'. He felt strange sensations of 'weight and pressure' inside his

*Political events during the last four years of his life, including the disastrous Russo-Japanese War of 1904, upset Rimsky deeply. In one of the demoralizing incidents of the war, the flagship of Admiral Makarov, the Petropavlovsk, struck a mine and sank, killing the admiral and 600 of those on board (above). Not only was Rimsky's patriotic pride affected but in an attempt to stem the tide of internal revolution – which was triggered by the war – the authorities cut the insurrection scene from the latest production of the opera Boris Godunov.*

that Balakirev became Director and with Rimsky as his assistant. The salary of 2300 rubles a year was certainly attractive to a man with a growing family – especially as Krabbe had been replaced and with him went the inspectorate of naval bands.

The old circle of friends was breaking up – only Borodin and Stasov were frequent visitors to the Rimsky-Korsakovs'. The new centre of activity was the home of Belyayev where students and trained musicians formed the core of the group. It was common for them to take off at one in the morning to have supper at a restaurant.

The death of Borodin in 1887 gave Rimsky-Korsakov the inheritance of *Prince Igor,* which needed finishing and orchestrating, a task which he set about with Glazunov in the spring. It was as though this task released his creative impulse and during the summer at Lake Nelay he composed the famous *Spanish Capriccio,* the first rehearsal of which was constantly interrupted by the orchestra's applause. This period of intense acclaim saw two further works of similar stature: the *Easter Overture* and *Scheherazade.* He was 44 and had just written three masterpieces, virtually one after the other.

### Descent into depression

After a trip to Brussels in 1890 he returned home to find Nadezhda seriously ill with diphtheria, a disease that soon infected his son Andrey. While the children were sent off to different homes in the country to cut the risk of further infection he noted sadly: 'The

head accompanied by various obsessive ideas which weighed him down and alarmed him. His brain continually played tricks on him and neurasthenia was eventually diagnosed – he was on the brink of a breakdown.

Masha too continued to decline. Nadezhda took her to the Crimea and Rimsky joined them later. He had a wretched time watching his daughter slowly dying while trying to uncloud his sick brain and spent much of that summer of 1893 writing harsh judgements on old friends in the *Record of my Musical Life*. On his way back to St. Petersburg he was overtaken by a telegram announcing Masha's death.

### Finest achievements

Rimsky-Korsakov was shaken out of this black period by the news of yet another death – that of Tchaikovsky, in October 1893 and he dedicated the first Russian Symphony Concert of the season to Tchaikovsky. Rimsky-Korsakov conducted this concert and even travelled to Odessa to conduct another memorial concert. Although he returned feeling better within himself – he found a new country house on Lake Pesno set in beautiful surrounding countryside – inspiration still seemed to be locked up inside him.

By 1897 he had regained his industrious driving force and *Sadko,* one of his finest achievements, was finished. This was followed by 40 or so songs, two duets, a cantata – the list goes on – but the direction was clear: it was away from nationalism towards, as he saw it, 'freedom of style'. In 1900, the 35th year of his career as composer was celebrated with concerts and presentations.

### The flames of revolution

The disastrous war with Japan in 1904 was a bitter blow to his patriotic feelings. Ever-worsening news from the front fanned the revolutionary flame throughout Russia and by January 1905 St Petersburg was virtually in a state of revolution. Even the Conservatoire's students, not known for their radicalism, were speaking out against the repressive tactics of the Director. The situation became critical and in March the building was surrounded by police, many of them mounted. Rimsky-Korsakov added his signature to a letter demanding the Director's resignation. The Director resigned, Rimsky-Korsakov was sacked, the Conservatoire closed down by the authorities. By publishing another letter deploring the situation and resigning his honorary membership to the Russian Music Society, Rimsky-Korsakov became, overnight, the hero of liberal Russia.

Things were brought to a head when the students gave a concert which soon turned into a political rally. The police, who broke up the concert, then had all of Rimsky-Korsakov's compositions banned and in one stroke ensured their lasting popularity when the ban was lifted after a few months. He let none of this go to his head however and once more he took up his memoirs. While the Conservatoire was closed he gave private lessons and even organized a concert in aid of the families of destitute workers. When it was reopened and he was invited back in 1906 it was for but a brief stay; he stormed out after another disagreement. That summer he took a holiday with his family on Lake Garda where he finished the *Record of my Musical Life*.

Within a few weeks of his return to St Petersburg he was hard at work on what was to be his last opera,

*The Golden Cockerel,* with a libretto by Bel'sky based on a Pushkin fairy tale. Before the end of 1906 the work was well under way.

At about this time the young Igor Stravinsky whom he had met a few years before and who was a regular at the Rimsky-Korsakov's Wednesday musical evenings became a pupil. The master-pupil relationship between them developed into deep friendship and Rimsky became a paternal figure for Stravinsky, whose own father had died in 1902.

In 1907 after conducting some of the Cinq Concerts Historiques Russes organized by Diaghilev in Paris, where he was confronted by the 'new and incomprehensible' music of Debussy, Scriabin and Strauss, he returned to Russia to spend the summer at the beautiful estate of Lyubensk. By mid-September the score of *The Golden Cockerel* was complete but the seemingly never ending problems with the censor over the libretto made the last months of his life all the more difficult. During the summer Rimsky received a letter from Glazunov who wanted to know if he would accept an honorary doctorate from Oxford or Cambridge. The answer was that he most certainly would not. However he was elected a corresponding member of the Academie des Beaux Arts.

In March 1908 his birthday was marred by stabbing pains in his chest. In April he had an attack of angina followed by a further attack five days later. He recovered sufficiently to go to Lyubensk in May. In the early hours of 12 June there was a violent thunderstorm after which he suffered another attack and died. After a service in the chapel of the St Petersburg Conservatoire he was buried in the cemetery of the Novodevichy Monastery.

*Following the defeat in the Russo-Japanese war, any elements of discontent which might have simmered below the surface in Russia now boiled up as revolutionary zeal. After the first major confrontation – Bloody Sunday, 9 January 1905 – when about 1000 people were killed when police fired on a peaceful demonstration in front of the Winter Palace in St Petersburg (below), Rimsky found himself in support of the grievances of students at the Conservatoire. He endorsed their activities in letters to the press and the Director. As a result Rimsky was dismissed, as the cartoon, left, shows.*

*Although idolized by his pupils and adored by his public, Rimsky-Korsakov (below) was a modest man and acutely aware of his own limitations.*

# Scheherazade, op. 35

**Rimsky-Korsakov based his colourful symphonic suite, Scheherazade, on the fairy-tale wonders of the Arabian Nights, hoping that the listener's fancy would follow a similar path to his own.**

*Scheherazade* is one of the most popular orchestral suites in the concert repertoire. It offers a brilliant kaleidoscope of sound and a richness of texture which appeal to both the imagination and the emotions. Its sparkling variety stems partly from the fantastic nature of its theme, and partly from the composer's supreme technical mastery of his instrumental forces.

During the summer of 1888 at the country estate of Nyherzhgovitsky, Rimsky had put the finishing touches to both *Scheherazade* and the *Russian Easter Overture*. These two works, along with the flamboyant *Capriccio Espagnol* composed the year before, summed up a vital stage in the composer's development. According to Rimsky, his works had 'now attained a considerable degree of virtuosity and warm sonority without Wagnerian influence'. He had achieved this by deliberately limiting himself to the 'normally constituted orchestra' of Glinka – the great forefather and inspiration of the Russian school of composers, known as the 'Mighty Handful'.

Glinka's two major stage works had been *A Life for the Tsar* and *Ruslan and Ludmilla*. The former was based on Russian history, while the latter was based upon a fairy-tale epic by Pushkin of the most wildly surreal king. These works provided the composer with a wonderfully diverse set of opportunities for original orchestral colouring, while allowing him to explore the exotic and fantastic elements in his Russian heritage. Both these seeds sown by Glinka were to bear fruit.

### Into the realms of fantasy

Following Glinka's lead, Rimsky produced a string of fantastic fairy-tale operas. These include *Snow Maiden* (1880), *Tsar Saltan* (1899), *Kashchey the Immortal* (1901-2), *Legend of the Invisible City of Kitzeh* (1903-5) and, the most famous of all, *The Golden Cockerel* (1906-7). It was *The Snow Maiden* that initially fired Rimsky's enthusiasm for 'ancient Russian customs and heathen pantheism' and induced him, in a state of great excitement, to explore the realms of fantasy. Composing feverishly in the depths of the countryside, he found himself praying to a gnarled tree stump or an ancient willow tree, and then at cockcrow 'scattering the sorcery of the night'.

*It sometimes seemed to me that animals, birds and even trees and flowers, know more of the magic and fantastic than human beings do . . . I warmly believed in all this as a child would.*

Rimsky's first purely orchestral work on a fairy-tale theme was *Skazka,* which literally means 'Fairy-tale'. *Skazka* had originally been called *Baba Yaga,* the name of the most terrifying witch of Russian folk-tales, but this very specific title was missing from the printed score of 1886. In his autobiography, Rimsky complains of the attempts by both critics and public to delineate precisely a narrative or pictorial quality throughout the work. He assured his reader that the effort is doomed to failure. Correspondingly, the story of the composition of *Scheherazade* was outlined by the composer in unusual detail. He stated that he had been guided by a programme in composing *Scheherazade,* but a programme consisting of separate episodes, rather than a straightforward narrative, and pictures from *The Thousand and One Nights:* the sea and Sinbad's ship; the fantastic account of the Kalender prince; the young prince and the young princess; the celebration at Baghdad; and the ship dashed upon a rock. The only unifying thread consisted of short introductions to the first, second, and fourth movements and an intermezzo in the third, all written for a solo violin and depicting the beautiful Scheherazade herself in the midst of telling her marvellous tales to the terrible sultan.

Of all the sources of myths and legends,

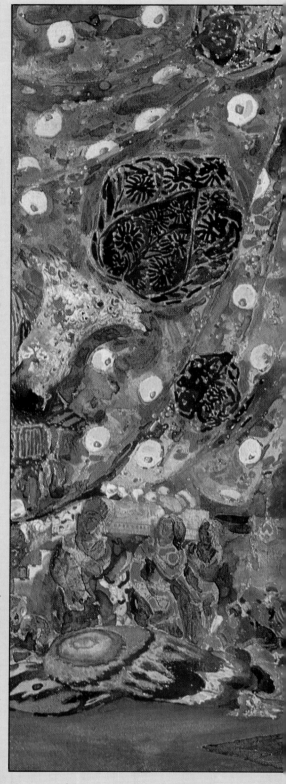

*In* Scheherazade *(title page – left), Rimsky-Korsakov created a dazzling oriental fantasy (above), rich in texture and pulsating with vibrant orchestral colour.*

*The One Thousand and-One Nights* is the collection *par excellence* which instantly conjures up images of oriental splendour. And tying himself loosely to this well known storyline, Rimsky has a head start in evoking a response of wonder and enchantment. On the flyleaf of the score there is even a précis of the central plot:

*The Sultan Schahriar, persuaded of the falseness and faithlessness of women, had sworn to put to death every one of his wives after the first night. But the Sultana Scheherazade saved her life by interesting him in the tales which she told him during a thousand and one nights. Driven by curiosity, the Sultan put off from day to day his wife's execution and ended by giving up his bloody decision completely. For her stories, the Sultana borrowed from poets their verses, from folksongs their words, and she interwove them with stories and adventures.*

Rimsky's comments on the interpretation of the work are strongly critical of those who wish to precisely translate the music back into narrative. It would be pointless to search in his suite for recurring themes or leading themes, (leit-

According to the fairy-tale, Scheherazade *(right)* – whose gentle presence permeates Rimsky's music – saved her life by telling magical tales to her husband, the Sultan Schahriar. Shahriar had resolved to marry and kill a new wife each day, but Scheherazade's stories were so entertaining that he delayed the day of execution and finally relented. The stories she told during a thousand and one nights, form the collection popularly known as the Arabian Nights *(centre right)*. Rimsky, with characteristic flair, used this source in an imaginative rather than a literal fashion.

Two years after Rimsky-Korsakov's death, Diaghilev's ballet company staged Scheherazade – for which Léon Bakst designed this sensuous Odalisque costume *(far right)*. The ballet only used three of the four movements of Rimsky's suite, and was based on an entirely different story-line – more erotic than exotic! Rimsky would certainly have not approved, judging by his reaction to the sensational dancer, Isadora Duncan: 'How vexed I should be', he wrote, 'if I learned that Miss Duncan danced and mimed to my Scheherazade, Antar or Easter Overture.'

my work I had in mind the creation of a suite in four movements, intimately linked by themes and common motifs, but presenting itself as a kaleidoscope of fabulous images of an oriental character . . .

The reference to a discussion concerning the titles given to each movement is particularly interesting:

*I even had the intention of calling Movement I of Scheherazade Prelude; II Ballade; III Adagio; and IV, Finale; but on the advice of Lyadov and others I held back from avoiding the attribution of an overly precise programme. Even so, in the new edition of the music I eventually destroyed all allusions to the programme*

which appeared in the titles of each part: *The Sea; Sinbad's Ship; The Kalender's Tale; etc.*

Lyadov counselled Rimsky well. Like the titles of Elgar's *Enigma Variations*, the movement 'labels' have prompted much concert-time conversation and speculation as listeners try to ferret out hidden references. This may not have seemed appropriate to the composer, but it had roused enough interest in the work to keep it before the public ever since its first appearance. Now that the suite is a firmly established favourite, it is possible to listen to the composer's very wise admonitions. After all, he had had his cake and eaten it!

*In composing* Scheherazade *I only wished*

motifs), always coherently linked to certain poetic ideas or images. On the contrary, Rimsky was confident that in most cases all these apparent leitmotifs were nothing but purely musical material. These themes permeate all the sections of the suite, following upon and interweaving with each other. Appearing each time under a different guise, they correspond in each instance to different images and to different narratives and pictures. Rimsky gives us an excellent example: the theme vigorously declaimed by the fanfare on muted trombone and trumpet, which first appears in the tale of the Kalender prince (second movement), reappears in the fourth movement in the depiction of the shipwreck, even though this episode has no logical place in the Kalender's narrative. Also the principal theme of the Kalender's tale and the princess's theme in the third movement appear, admittedly with a different emphasis and in a quicker tempo, as secondary themes in the festival of Baghdad, although in the stories of *The Arabian Nights* nothing is said about these characters participating in the merry-making. Finally, and perhaps the best example, the unison phrase which seems to depict Scheherazade's dreadful husband at the beginning of the suite appears in the story of the Kalender prince in which there cannot be any question of the appearance of the Sultan Schahriar. Rimsky comments:

*Thus, developing in a completely free manner the basic musical materials of*

Today, with an ever-increasing number of jumbo-jets circling the skies, the word 'Oriental' is likely to bring to mind the Far East of China, Japan and the Pacific islands of Indonesia and the Philippines; but in earlier times the Orient began rather closer to home. Indeed, the beginnings of Western European music lay in the chants and dances of the early Christians, which they 'borrowed' from Jewish traditions of worship around the Eastern coasts of the Mediterranean. With the polarization of the Christian church around the twin centres of Rome and Constantinople, the traditions of East and West developed in different directions. Another factor which contributed largely to the definition of the description 'Eastern' was the presence in large areas of Eastern Europe of the 'Infidel' — the rival civilization of the Muslim Turks, who actually reached the walls of Vienna in 1683, and who up until the early years of this century were considered one of the great powers of Europe.

The Turks' musical influence began, appropriately enough, in the sphere of military music. Turkish corps of 'janissaries', as the military bandsmen were known, were famous for their strongly percussive music, with so many instruments clashing on the first beat of every bar it was virtually impossible to march out of step. In the early 18th century, these bands attracted the attention of the rival European armies and Augustus II of Poland received a full Turkish military band as a gift from the Sultan; the Empress Anne of Russia then demanded one too and a troupe of a dozen players were despatched to her court. The Turkish performers retained their colourful novelty value for many

by these indications to steer the imagination of the listener a little along the path where my own fancy had wandered. I simply wanted the listener, if my symphonic music pleased him, to have the clear impression that it was about an oriental tale and not just four pieces played one after the other and based upon common themes.

His success in this suite must be judged partly on the ever-popular nature of Scheherazade in the concert hall. In the west, the musical public is far more aware of Rimsky as a symphonic composer than as a great musical dramatist, but the ever-green Scheherazade seems to hold both drama and orchestral virtuosity. The title of the suite might seem to belie Rimsky's defence, but he is very convincing in his insistence:

Why then does my suite carry the name Scheherazade? This is because this name and the title The Thousand and One Nights evoke the Orient and its marvellous stories for everyone. And

besides, certain details in the musical interpretation make reference to the fact that all these stories are told by the same person — and this person is Scheherazade.

## Programme notes

On the autograph orchestral score there was planned the following note, which, however, did not appear in the published copy:

The composer did not cling to an interlineary reproduction of any single fairy-tale, leaving it to the listener to find out by himself the images at which the programme hints.

Rimsky uses a relatively small orchestra considering the wealth of effects he produced. Glinka's orchestra was made up of 2 flutes, 2 oboes, 2 clarinets, 2 bassoons, contrabassoon, 4 horns, 2 trumpets, 3 trombones, kettledrums and strings. Rimsky adds colourful highlighting instruments, namely piccolo, English horn, bass tuba,

*The adventures of the 'wandering' Kalender prince occupy the second movement of Scheherazade. Here, Rimsky takes the idea of 'journeying' (above left) which features so strongly throughout the suite — whether by land or by sea.*

# *Understanding music: the oriental influence*

years, gradually becoming absorbed by European military bands and also finding their way into the concert-hall and the opera house. Mozart in particular was quick to make use of their percussive effects in his opera *Die Entführung aus dem Serail* (set in the Sultan's harem), and in the famous *Rondo alla Turca* from the A major piano sonata.

But Austria was not the only European country who was to benefit from artistic connections with the East. The 'Mighty Handful' of Russian composers who established so positively the Nationalist ideals which burgeoned during the mid-19th century needed to look no further than the Asiatic provinces of their own country, and the strongly characterized melodies of their native folk-song. If there is one adjective which characterizes the music of Borodin, Mussorgsky, Rimsky-Korsakov and their fellows more than any other, it is 'colourful'. These composers were able to create the rich tapestries of oriental sound often from first-hand experience; a visit to the Suther provinces, the Caucasus or the Crimea, would provide first-hand knowledge of the Muezzin's dawn call to prayer and the sultry heat of the day which, together with the native mournfulness of the Russian temperament, inspired the creation of *Scheherazade* and the Polovtsian Dances from *Prince Igor*.

Elsewhere the Oriental stimulus was provided rather more commercially, by trading connections. The French fashion for 'Chinoiseries' went hand in hand with the colonizing of South-East Asia and influenced the visual as well as the performing arts. Eastern fashions in music began, as so often in France, in the opera-

*Ludwig Sievert's costume design for 'King Altoum' in Puccini's opera* Turandot.

house, with oriental legends like Délibes' *Lakmé* and Bizet's *Pearl-Fishers*. But the event which was to have the most profound and lasting impact on the progress of French music (and developments elsewhere) was the appearance at the Paris World Exhibition of 1889 of a Javanese 'Gamelan'. 'Gamelan' is a generic term for a group of tuned gongs, chimes and xylophone-type instruments. The performances in Paris had a lasting influence on the music of both Debussy and Ravel. Debussy, in particular, found elements of repetition and variation which provided an alternative structure to the Germanic treatment

of developing themes found in the traditional forms of symphony and sonata.

Paris in the early 1900s was also the venue for another colourful spectacle imported from further East — Diaghilev's 'Ballets Russes', whose exotic productions, often to new scores composed by leading composers of the day (among them, of course, Stravinsky), initiated a new era in both dance and music. The vogue set by Diaghilev was taken up once again in opera, with the greatest success being achieved by Puccini with *Turandot* and *Madame Butterfly*.

In recent years, many composers have turned increasingly towards the East, not only for inspiration but also seeking new techniques and new sound-worlds. Music, like speech, communicates through many languages; where verbal languages differ in vocabulary and grammar from one linguistic group to another, those of music use different pitches, scales and rhythms to create their own native character. The Western musical tradition familiar to us today happens to organize pitch into 12 equal semitones — from which are derived the familiar major and minor scales and, more recently, the 12-note rows of contemporary serial music — and rhythm into units of two or three beats which can be grouped together to form more complex patterns, usually within a regular rhythmic pulse. But this is the grammar of just one language, and there are many other scales, rhythms and instruments, some primitive some sophisticated, which form the basis of a variety of different musical languages. These exotic sounds will undoubtedly continue to be a source of fascination to Western composers.

*In the third movement — the story of the young prince and the young princess — Rimsky indulges in some wonderfully lyrical writing for orchestra. The tender, amorous melody, with its slightly wistful beauty, conjures up a picture of lovers gently embracing (left).*

snare drums, bass drum, tambourine, cymbals, harp and triangle.

### 1 The Sea and Sinbad's ship
**Largo e maestoso — Lento – Allegro non troppo**
This movement opens with a dramatic fanfare on trombones, a dark, menacing theme played in octaves.

Example 1

Rimsky with his usual insistence, warns against identifying this majestic theme too closely with the stern Sultan, Schahriar. The quiet woodwinds which follow appear to pacify the forbidding opening motif. Out of this calm appears the lovely violin solo theme associated with the narrator, who (as Rimsky says) 'happens to be Scheherazade'.

Example 2

*At the heart of the final movement of Scheherazade, Rimsky depicts a violent scene of shipwreck (right). As the waves swell, and the skies darken, the composer summons up all his orchestral resources. In a dramatic climax, with clashing cymbals suggesting the crash of mighty waves, Sinbad's ship is driven against the rocks.*

Albert Goodwin 'Shipwreck'. The Tate Gallery

This theme is accompanied by the harp on its initial entry. A third thematic element is a simple rocking accompaniment in the lower part of the orchestra, suggestive of waves at sea or gentle travelling. This musical element returns in the 'shipwreck' in the fourth movement, but in a more agitated and violent form. The full orchestra divides to balance this rocking bass line against the lyrical melody carried by the upper strings. A tranquil section is introduced by plucked strings with solo sections for woodwind and horn. The cellos continue the rocking figure. After another violin solo, the full orchestra enters restating the principal themes in a denser texture with timpani expanding both orchestral complexity and volume. Another quiet section follows with solos for violins, flute, and clarinet with a sustaining accompaniment by the horn. The violins have more complicated figurations. The full orchestra again returns, swelling the sound. A feeling of great lyrical intensity builds as the trumpets and piccolo enrich the orchestral colouring. Once again, a section marked *tranquillo* features clarinet and violin solos of considerable virtuosity. This section is very short and leads immediately to a thundering conclusion for the full orchestra. A final reminiscence of the calm of 'Scheherazade's' lovely violin theme in the coda (or tail-piece) of the movement is accompanied by gently plucked (pizzicato) strings.

## 2 The story of the Kalender prince
### Lento
Kalenders were wandering dervishes, and this movement continues Rimsky's preoccupation with 'journeying' throughout the suite. The Scheherazade theme opens the movement in another expressive violin solo, marked *lento* or slowly. Then an *andantino* (again the idea of walking) on the solo bassoon, leads to the next 'tale'. The bassoon's theme is echoed by the oboe, but this time with harp accompaniment. Now the full orchestra concentrates on this theme, but at a faster tempo. The graceful melody is supported by *pizzicato* (plucked) strings. The violin and oboe again converse quietly before a very fast section is introduced by the brass. First the trombone enters with a theme of alarm.

Example 3

This is echoed by the trumpet and announces a fierce musical conflict, which conjures up images of many of the fairy-tale adventures of martial deeds. The strings shudder as the brass become louder and the cymbals clash. A clarinet solo, and then quick cries from the woodwind, lead to a march-like variation on the brass theme. Once again the bassoon has a solo before the element of conflict returns. Scheherazade's theme reappears in the bottom register of the orchestra, but this time in a

martial guise. The harp and the brass are now in opposition. Soon, the harp and flute combine to bring a momentary sense of peace. Then the brass sounds quietly in contrast to the solo violin. To end the 'tale', the full orchestra builds to a speedy and crashing conclusion.

## 3 The young prince and the young princess
### Andantino quasi allegretto
This movement begins with what might be termed 'the princess's theme' played on the violins.

Example 4

It is a gentle, amorous melody with a slightly melancholy beauty. Rippling decorations on clarinets and flutes punctuate the central melody's repetitions. The atmosphere is very dream-like, and reminiscent of Debussy – another composer intrigued by the Orient.

Suddenly, a jaunty clarinet tune interrupts this languid melody. The orchestral colour is changed with the addition of side drum, triangle, tambourine and timpani. Trombones also enter, but softly. The march which ensues seems to be a light-hearted ceremonial procession, accompanied by plucked and muted strings. Soon, the dreamy opening melody returns and the oboe repeats its sweet solo. It is answered by a violin solo with another

variation of Scheherazade's theme. The orchestra swells the lyrical theme again. The march theme reappears, but now as a lyrical dance with much emphasis on the tuneful strings. A flute solo provides a bridge to the playful conclusion with its exotic orchestration – another variation on the joyful oriental procession at the heart of this section.

### 4 The festival at Baghdad; The sea; The ship goes to pieces against a rock surmounted by a bronze warrior
### Allegro molto – Allegro molto – Lento – Vivo – Allegro non troppo e maestoso

The orchestra immediately bounces into activity with an excited, bubbling theme. A violin solo briefly interrupts with a gentle reminder of Scheherazade's slow theme supported by the harp. Then the full orchestra continues its 'frenetic' activity (*Allegro molto e frenetico*) conjuring up the noise and colour of the festival at Baghdad. The lively sounds of percussion (timpani, triangle, tambourine and cymbals) heighten the sense of exotic celebration. Again the violin soloist seems to restrain the joy in a slow cadenza – acting like a musical brake. Then a gentle drumming rhythm accompanies a lilting melody that starts up on the flute.

More and more instruments join in the accompaniment to this melody and many themes from earlier movements recur, including the themes of the young prince and the Kalender prince. There is a clash of tempi and rhythms as the frenzy increases. Brass calls intertwine with the woodwind. Cymbal clashes punctuate the wild dance-rhythms.

The percussion and the rising and falling figures on the strings soon explode into the broad sea melody of the first movement with cymbals conjuring up the splash of gigantic waves. Flute and piccolo plus upper strings create a delightful impression of flurrying winds. This movement is the most explicitly pictorial of the four. A moment of stasis provides an even more dramatic orchestral detonation as the musical ship smashes against the rock surmounted by the bronze warrior. Rimsky uses sustained notes, especially in the brass, to graphically portray the hollow echoing statue.

Calm follows the storm. The gentle rocking accompaniment returns. The Scheherazade melody appears with harp for the last time. The music echoes the satisfying conclusion of *The Thousand and One Nights* itself, where, by using feminine guile and persuasion Scheherazade has averted the doom which had hung over her. As her harp melody fades the long-held notes on the violin emphasize this gentle but triumphant ending. Like the heroine herself the music spreads a sweet atmosphere of peace.

## Great interpreters

### Seiji Ozawa (conductor)

Ozawa was born in 1935 in Manchuria. His parents were both Japanese, and he was introduced to Western music by his Christian mother. Consequently, he started learning piano at the age of seven.

The family moved to Tokyo and in 1951 he entered the Toho School of Music, studying composition and conducting under Saito, as well as continuing on the piano. However, an accident to two of his fingers during a game of rugby ended any hope of a concert career as a pianist, and he concentrated on conducting. By 1954 he had conducted the NHK and the Japanese PO, but scarcity of opportunity finally drove him from Japan to Europe, where in Paris he resumed his studies, this time under Bigot. The move was a shrewd one, for in 1959 he won the International Young Conductors' Competition. After this success, Charles Munch invited him to study at Tanglewood, Mass., and within a year of his arrival he had been awarded a Koussevitzky Memorial Scholarship. In 1961 he made his Western début as a conductor at Carnegie Hall.

That same year he won another scholarship to study under Karajan in Berlin, and while he was there he met Bernstein. Bernstein hired him as assistant conductor on a tour of Japan, a post he retained back in New York. Between 1963 and 1965 he

*Seiji Ozawa conducting (above).*

Phonogram International

held a number of minor posts before winning an appointment as musical director of the Toronto SO, a position he held for three years until 1968. His next post was as musical director of the San Francisco SO, from 1970 to 1975.

During these years, Ozawa had been appointed joint artistic director of Tanglewood, where he took charge of the Boston Symphony Orchestra's festival concerts. By 1972 he had become the orchestra's adviser, and in 1973 he was made their music director, a post he still holds. He has subsequently toured and recorded extensively with the orchestra. In the meantime he still fulfils many guest engagements and conducted the first performance of Messiaen's *St. Francis of Assisi* in Paris in 1983.

### FURTHER LISTENING

#### Symphony no. 2 ('Antar')

Rimsky-Korsakov worked intermittently on revising his second symphony for over 30 years, unsatisfied as he was with his youthful effort at symphonic form. He finally published it for the last time in 1903 as a symphonic suite. In this designation he seems to have been correct, for the work, written originally as the classic four-movement symphony, is in fact no symphony in strict definition, lacking the formal design and essential carrying-through of ideas which is at the very core of symphonic writing. But as a suite it is an imaginative and highly enjoyable piece of orchestral writing, full of youthful verve and enthusiasm.

#### The Golden Cockerel Suite

*The Golden Cockerel* was the composer's last completed opera, intended for performance in the 1906/7 concert season. However, due to a government ban on the work, given its fantasy theme of the irresponsibility brought about by the exercise of absolute power, the composer never saw it performed. Nevertheless, Rimsky did hear the suite which he had arranged in an attempt to generate interest and publicity for the work – and it is the suite, a wonderful collection of interludes and themes, which is most often heard today.

# IN THE BACKGROUND

# 'Mysterious East'

## *The burning desert, the bustle of bazaars and the secret world of the harem all conjured up an exotic picture of the East and gave rise to a cult of Orientalism that was to influence the arts of Europe.*

Fascinating, colourful, mysterious and exotic – this was the popular notion of the 'Orient' that excited so many 19th-century Europeans. Fed by the backflow of romanticized images, along avenues laid open by the Great Powers' imperialist ventures, they thrilled to the world of *Scheherazade* and *Arabian Nights.*

The influence of the Orient – in this sense the lands of North Africa and the Near East – struck a resounding chord, particularly in Britain and France, manifesting itself in the cult of Orientalism promoted by writers, artists, archaeologists and tourists alike.

Yet it was not only the seemingly unchanging exotic idea of the Orient that prevailed. Just as Europe had once looked back to the extinct classicism of Greece and Rome, so too the once glorious empire of Islam appeared romantically attractive in its decay.

### The decline of an empire

In the 7th century the Arabs erupted from the Arabian Peninsula to spread Islam through North Africa, the Near East and Southern Europe in an amazingly rapid series of conquests. The gains were eventually whittled away by the counterattacks of Christendom and the Mongol invasions. The decline of Muslim Arab power made room for the rise of Muslim Turkish power so that over the centuries almost the whole extent of the Arab empire came under Turkish rule.

By the end of the 18th century Turkish power was also in decline. The Ottoman Turkish Sultan reigned in Istanbul but his control over various disparate parts of his empire was really only nominal. His agent in Egypt was the Pasha but real power rested in the hands of the Mamluks, an aristocratic warrior caste of slave descent. In the Western Mediterranean the Dey of Algiers recognized that the Sultan was his overlord but was, nevertheless, virtually an independent ruler.

It was soon to become painfully apparent that none of these Muslim potentates could remotely match the military strength of the major powers of Western Europe. Their inadequacy was pitilessly demonstrated by Napoleon's invasion of Egypt in 1798 which resulted in a crushing defeat for the army of the Mamluks. In the next year the Sultan sent an Ottoman army to the Nile to drive the French out but this was also defeated by Napoleon. In the end the Muslim East was saved from conquest by the French through the unwelcome agency of the British who destroyed the French fleet at Abu Qir Bay in August 1798.

While the European powers occupied their strength in the Napoleonic Wars the Muslim Orient had a breathing space. This time was used in a futile attempt to build up military power and industrial strength in order to match and combat the European invaders. The Sultan revived his power over Anatolia, Syria, Palestine and the Hijaz and in a brutal drastic attempt to found a modern army, organized the massacre of his janissary corps in 1826.

*Involvement in the East by Europeans had its roots in commercial exploitation, and countries were prepared to fight to protect their interests – as did Britain and France at Abu Qir Bay (below).*

Lejeune 'Battle of Abu Qir'. Versailles. Photo Bulloz

*The romantic 19th-century European view of the Orient centred on the 'nobility' of the native people, particularly the Bedouin, who were seen to represent the pure and uncorrupt element – the lords of the burning sand – of a civilization and empire in decay.*

In Egypt the military adventurer Muhammed Ali seized power in 1805 and treacherously murdered the Mamluks whom he had invited to feast in the Cairo Citadel. Muhammed Ali founded a Khedivial dynasty and also took pains to encourage new industries and remodel his army. It was all in vain. The whole of the Orient was to come under pressure from the developed countries of Europe, whose growing industrial power was the most potent agent of imperialism in history.

### Imperial expansion

Industrialization had brought wealth and technical sophistication to those countries that were able to exploit resources and from this new found wealth developed massive military might. For much of the 19th century the supreme power was Great Britain which had an unrivalled manufacturing capacity and wealth enough to overwhelm and beggar the undeveloped nations of the world. British exports to Turkey and the Middle East rose from £3.5 million in

*Wealthy European countries financed many major expensive projects, including the Suez canal (below). Unfortunately, the recipient countries were rarely able to repay the heavy debts incurred and thus had little choice but to accept government by their creditors. In this way, Britain, for example, was able to exercise firm control over Egypt.*

being nervous of possible Russian threats to the Indian Empire. The British task of preserving Turkey's independence was made fairly easy by Russian backwardness, the splendid fighting qualities of Turkish soldiers and Britain's own great wealth and naval power. This sterile duel between Russia and Britain only came to real war when the French tried to join this imperial contest. France had been quiet for some time after Waterloo but the revival of their Empire under Napoleon III in 1852 made them eager to seek glory and prestige abroad — partly to distract attention from domestic troubles. The French had invaded Algeria in 1830, initially to suppress piracy there; in the next two decades they began systematic colonization with European settlers. Military commanders on the spot began to expand French territory, sometimes against orders from the government in Paris.

Such military adventurism alarmed the British — as did Napoleon's claim to be the guardian of Catholic monks in the Holy Land, and French interference in Syria in 1860. Predictably, such

*First moves to colonize Algeria began in 1830, but it was not until 18 years later that it was declared French territory. French travellers were enticed into visiting their new and exotic province as this Parisian poster shows (above).*

*Sir Richard Burton (above right) was the most notable Arabist of his time. He translated many great Arabic works including his famous 16-volume annotated edition of the Arabian Nights.*

1848 to £16 million in 1870 — a huge increase which was enormous by the standards of the time. At times this trade was forcibly imposed upon weak, non-European countries, most noticeably in the Chinese Opium War (1840-42). This war forced the Chinese imperial government to allow unrestricted entry of all British goods — including opium — into China, with devastating consequences for the Chinese. Generally, however, there was little need to force British goods on to countries — they were eager to import far more than they could afford. They then became saddled with huge debts, which could lead to a loss of real independence.

The threat posed by powerful European economies was made even more dire by the political rivalry between the European powers. In the Middle East, the basic equation was that Turkey was always threatened by Russia which wished to partition her or turn her into a puppet state. On the other hand, Russian ambitions were naturally opposed by Britain,

exploits led to Anglo-French rivalry which was not eased when the British occupied Egypt. Unfortunately for the Egyptians they were almost predestined to fall into the British sphere because they were an important supplier of cotton to British mills and occupied a strategically important position on the globe which was further enhanced when the Suez canal was completed in 1869.

The British attack on Egypt followed the classic pattern of British imperialism. Muhammed Ali's successors had not been as resourceful as he or as financially prudent. His grandson Ismail borrowed heavily in Europe to finance railways, ports, telegraph networks, fleets of steamships and the Suez Canal. By 1879 the Egyptian treasury was bankrupt so Ismail was deposed and his successor Tewfitz forced to accept government by the Public Debt Administration which was composed of Europeans. In 1881 the Egyptian Army revolted against this alien rule but was promptly defeated by a British expedi-

*So strong was their fascination with the East that some hardy and adventurous orientalists decided to make it their home. Lady Jane Ellenborough (top) married a Bedouin sheikh – her fourth husband. Lady Hester Stanhope (above) was crowned 'Queen of the Desert'.*

*The colour and bustle of a busy Arab street (right) lived up to the romantic expectations of 19th-century European travellers.*

tionary force. From then on the Khedivs ruled as British puppets and, when the Anglo-Egyptian Army invaded and subdued the Sudan, this was an extension of British not Egyptian power.

By this time other European powers were proving eager to scramble for imperial gains. Italy, Belgium and Germany had come late to the race and the urgency with which they prosecuted their ambitions made all the Europeans powers behave like sharks when there is blood in the water. It had been demonstrated to the satisfaction of the Europeans concerned that the natives were incapable of managing their own affairs so that it was time to take up the white man's burden and govern them for their own good.

## Lords of the desert

For the romantic Orientalists all this was quite easy to understand. The peoples of the Orient were a colourful but corrupt crowd who could not stand out against progress but needed shepherding along the right paths by 'superior' Europeans. There were,

however, a few — most of them highly eccentric — who could accept the general theory of this but maintained that an uncorrupted elite still existed and eventually this elite would provide uncorrupt and worthy Muslim rulers. The people they referred to were the Bedouin.

In 1754, the philosopher Jean Jacques Rousseau had published his *Discourse on the Origins and Foundations of Inequality Among Men*. His vision was to have a longstanding, widespread and powerful appeal, especially to those who were determined to fasten a highly romantic character upon the Bedouin. There was already some evidence that they were not entirely the murderous cut-throats that travellers had traditionally found them to be. Laurent D'Arvieux, an Arabic-speaking Englishman, managed to make himself an honoured guest in Bedouin tents as early as 1664 and he reported most favourably on their hospitality and honesty. This description touched some chord in Europeans who wanted to believe in a faithful, honest and manly race who were literally gentlemen of the desert.

But as the Bedouin in general failed to measure up to the highly romanticized opinion Europeans held of them it was not long before some intrepid travellers set off in search of the 'real thing' — pure Bedouin who could be counted upon to fit the image! Jean Louis Burckhardt, a dangerously unobservant Swiss, was the first to make the terrible journey into the

Musee des Beaux-Arts, Nantes

*Many aspects of Oriental life were sensationalized for the benefit of the 19th-century European market. Paintings such as* A Purchase for the Harem *(above left) gave people preconceived notions as to what life in the East was like – notions which, for the most part, were highly exaggerated. The portrait of* The White Slave *(above) was painted in 1888 – nearly 30 years after the slave trade had been banned by the Ottoman Sultan. Peeps into the secret and sensual world of the harem (left), whether true to life or not, were immensely popular, appealing as they did to the more voyeuristic Europeans – whose fascination with Turkey survived an age old hostility.*

heart of the Arabian Peninsula. Disguised as 'Sheikh Ibrahim', a poor scholar of Cairo, he suffered desperate hardship and appalling danger on travels which included a visit to Mecca – certain death if his real identity had been discovered. During the trip he spent little or no time with the Bedouin themselves but did not hesitate to describe them as fiercely independent people who lived by a code of honour and who were both proud and patriotic.

By this time belief in the acceptability and gentlemanliness of the Bedouin was universal in Europe. The people of the towns of the Orient were, of course, regarded as decadent sensualists but it was a liberating thought for certain Europeans who were regarded as eccentric and therefore social 'misfits'. Here at last was an alternative society composed of a natural nobility in which they could surely find their niche. The most dazzling of these was probably the English woman, Lady Hester Stanhope, who had suffered something of a social eclipse at home and ventured east in 1811. Her obvious wealth and liberal use of it made her a very popular figure – so much so, that within a year she was crowned 'Queen of the Desert' at Palmyra. She became somewhat obsessed by Arab claims to nobility and concerned herself in proving that British aristocratic families were of Arab descent. But sadly, when her money ran out so did the warmth of her reception. She died old, poor and deserted in Lebanon in 1839.

Lady Ellenborough was rather more fortunate in her experiences of the East. Regarded in her youth as being somewhat featherbrained and loose-moralled, her final years in the Orient earned her an altogether different reputation. Her way East lay through Paris, Munich and Athens and included four husbands and countless lovers before she arrived in Syria in 1853. After a couple of affairs with Arab 'sheikhs' (titled English ladies tended to assume that all their oriental lovers were sheikhs and, therefore, aristocrats) she eventually married a member of the el Mezrab Bedouin. It would be unkind and quite possibly incorrect to suspect that her husband was attracted by her enormous income of £3000 a year because their marriage was a great success. The former Lady Ellenborough became an authority on Bedouin life and mores; the great British Arabist, Richard Burton described her as the cleverest woman he had ever met.

The interesting point about Lady Ellenborough's marriage to Medjuel el Mezrab was in the attitude of her fellow Europeans towards it. It would be an exaggeration to say that her Bedouin husband was acceptable – indeed her family would have been horrified if he had arrived in England – but he, however, was more acceptable than an English workman might have been. To people like Burton there was no question that she had made a mésalliance. The romantic view of the Bedouin had come so far that they were regarded as the true aristocracy of the Orient. Their life in the desert, hunting and raiding, was the equivalent of the proper gentleman's life in England's shires pursuing the fox.

Oddly enough this rather superficial idea of Bedouin character was to survive the investigation of the 19th century's most noted Arabists – and in particular Richard Burton. Burton was a quarrelsome man of violent emotions but, in his way, a genius who could pass as an Arab himself and driven by an insatiable curiosity about all things oriental. In 1853 he too made the pilgrimage to Mecca disguised as a Pathan. Any non-believer who went to Mecca

BBC Hulton Picture Library

faced real danger as discovery meant certain death. But it is probably true to say that Burton was safer than most such travellers because his knowledge of the East and gift of languages made his disguise virtually perfect. He was a complex character whose rather jumbled outlook on life was flavoured by fervent imperialism and a dedicated racialism. On the pseudo-scientific racial scale he employed, the Arabs of the Hijaz scored very highly and were evidently superior to the Egyptians or other 'degenerate' types at the 'most superficial glance'. Unfortunately for the Arabs of the Hijaz he considered them racially admirable but not up to the standard of the apogee of races, the English. Nonetheless, Burton was very concerned that the British Empire be extended to include the oriental peoples.

Others who spent much time among the Arab people concurred with Burton's idea that those of the Hijaz were a natural aristocracy among them. The poet Wilfred Scawen Blunt made many trips east in the 1870s. In contrast to Burton he was an anti-imperialist but, incongruously, a sort of feudalist and anti-democrat. He believed in government by aristocracy and, as far as the Arabs were concerned, he reckoned their most suitable aristocracy to be the family of the Sherifs of Mecca. Charles Doughty who lived among the Bedouin virtually as a beggar in the same era as Blunt left a far less slanted account of them — having seen both good and bad sides. He remembered with great tenderness their endurance of poverty and hardship and that, although desert hospitality might be sometimes grudgingly given, it was amazing that such poor people gave it at all.

While British travellers such as these sought desert experiences in the Hijaz, the French became intoxicated with their new province of Algeria. The immense size of the waste was awe-inspiring, and the light, the aridity and the colour of the rolling desert were entirely new experiences.

*Only the very brave or the very reckless European dared make the pilgrimage to Mecca (above), the birthplace of the prophet Muhammed. Discovery of non-believers (i.e. non-Muslims) meant certain death.*

*By the end of the 19th century Thomas Cook's Egyptian tours were well established. His famous paddle steamers (an illustration from a passenger list is shown on the right) took many European tourists up the Nile to experience the wonders of the Sphinx and the pyramids (above right).*

Cook's Nile Service

M. S. " HATASOO "

## A tourist spectacle

Most of the fashion for Orientalism was fed, however, by enthusiasm for softer images than those afforded by the desert and its hardy nomads. The tales of the *Arabian Nights* had first been translated into French in 1704 and a series of English translations began after 1740. By the end of the 18th century it had become almost universally acknowledged and loved in Europe as a child's story book. Most of the tales do not concern the desert so much as the cities of the Orient. They deal with such exotica as Caliphs and harems, slaves and executioners; things which to adult Europeans seemed erotic with their undertones of sex and cruelty.

Although there was a certain fashion for orientalism among those who never went near the Levant or North Africa, for others nothing would do but a trip East to see the fabulous world of genies and bazaars themselves. Where only a hardy few had ventured at the beginning of the 19th century many now pressed, and the tourist industry was soon in full swing. Murray's *Handbook for Travellers in the Ionian Islands, Greece, Turkey, Asia Minor and Constantinople* first appeared in 1840, the volume for Egypt in 1847. The Librairie Hachette's *Itineraire descriptif, historique et archaeologique de l'Orient* was published in 1861. Baedecker guides soon followed and Thomas Cook began Egyptian tours in 1869. By 1880 Cook's had control of its famous Nile paddle steamers. The Orient was well on the way to being tamed and presented as a tourist spectacle.

*The vogue of Orientalism extended beyond the realms of culture and into the world of European fashion (above).*

*The romantic and fanciful obsession with things Eastern sometimes reached absurd proportions. Brighton pavilion (left) re-built in the early 19th century is a fine example of Orientalism run riot.*

John W. Considine, Jr. presents

# RUDOLPH VALENTINO
## in "The Son of the Sheik"
### a Sequel to 'The Sheik'
#### with VILMA BANKY
from the novel by E.M. HULL — Adapted to the Screen by FRANCES MARION
A GEORGE FITZMAURICE PRODUCTION
- UNITED ARTISTS PICTURE -

*Europe's fascination with the exotic East lived on into the 20th century and it was not long before the movie moguls moved in to promote and cash-in on it. Rudolph Valentino, 'screen lover' of the 1920s was undoubtedly the most famous 'sheikh' of them all. He died in 1926 at the height of his popularity – the year the above film was released.*

For many of those who travelled expecting to find scenes straight from the pages of the *Arabian Nights* they had read as children, the experience proved satisfying. In fact, in 1846 Thackeray's exultant advice to those who had loved the *Arabian Nights* in their youth was to 'book themselves on board one of the Peninsular & Orient vessels and try one dip into Constantinople or Smyrna. Walk into the bazaar, and the East is unveiled to you'. And Disraeli wrote: 'The meanest merchant in the bazaar looks like a Sultan in an Eastern fairy tale'. The artists of the Orientalist school frequently reflected this pleasure at finding a world that had stood still in time when they painted street scenes or bazaars. But for sensation seeking Europeans – those for whom the *Arabian Nights* conjured up an entirely different picture – the East was not unchanging and some of them resented it. After a tour of Egypt Mark Twain wrote:

*The great slave markets we have read so much about – where tender young girls were stripped for inspection, and criticized and discussed just as if they were horses at an agricultural fair – no longer exist.*

His obvious disappointment reflected the darker side of Occidental preoccupations which projected European – or, indeed, American – interest in lust and cruelty on to the 'degenerate' population of the Levant or North Africa. In 1846 pressure from Christian missions closed the Tunis slave market and in 1854-55 the Ottoman Sultan prohibited the white slave trade, and two years later the black slave trade. Despite this it was hard to convince Westerners that slavery and prostitution were not rife in the Orient. In 1834 all *Almahs* or prostitutes were banned from Cairo, much to the chagrin of the French writer Flaubert who had to seek them out in the provincial towns of Egypt. Prostitutes, exotic dancers, slaves and odalisques – oppressed women schooled to gratify a man's grossest whim – were an important part of the Occident's 'view' of the Orient.

## Influences on art and literature

In drawing on this view of the Orient, the art and literature of 19th-century Europe reflected a rather untruthful image of the Orient. This is not to say that everything produced was of low quality or unworthy. Edward FitzGerald's *Rubaiyat of Omar Khayyam,* a free and personal re-creation from the original Persian, first saw the light of day in 1859. FitzGerald had never been to the Orient yet his work was a polished vehicle for spreading the ingenuous, romantic view of the East; but it was also great poetry. Richard Burton's annotated version of the *Arabian Nights* merely reinforced western prejudices with its detailed speculation upon Arab character and the erotic side of life in the Levant. Upon its publication in 1886 the *Edinburgh Review* commented: 'Probably no European has ever gathered such an appalling collection of degrading customs and statistics of vice' – the sort of review which helped the book achieve almost best-seller status. Yet Burton's desire was to inform, not tickle prurient fancies. It was simply unfortunate that western readers were more interested in the sexually titillating parts of his work rather than in the main body of serious research.

This sort of consideration applied to an even greater extent in Orientalist painting. The luxury and sensuality of some elements of Oriental life gave artists a ready excuse to produce highly commercial 'sexy' pictures. However, Orientalism was not simply exploited by all the artists it touched and it would be invidious to single out one from the numbers of Germans, Italians, French and Britons who painted Eastern life with genuine humanity and conviction – of course their paintings were not so easily sold as those with more sensational themes.

As the effect of Orientalism upon Art varied with the perception of each artist, the same could be said of literature and, with the theories and writings of the Arabists, of sociology and anthropology. Although there was much honest endeavour which reflected much that was true there was also much that was meretricious and shallow, which exposed the truth about the corruption of a society. Ironically the society that was corrupt was not only, that of the Orient but equally that of the Occident – but in the latter case the corruption stemmed from its own power and sense of superiority.

## THE GREAT COMPOSERS

# Sergei Rachmaninov

## (1873–1943)

*Sergei Rachmaninov was not only the last composer in the tradition of Russian Romanticism, but one of the world's great piano virtuosos. He was trained at the Moscow Conservatoire and soon afterwards won acclaim for both his warm, melodic compositions and his skills as a concert pianist. He toured the United States as both a conductor and as a virtuoso, enjoying equal success in both roles. Rachmaninov did not adhere to the nationalist ideals of the 'Mighty Handful', instead looking to Tchaikovsky and the 19th century Romantic movement to influence his works. The Romantic traditions of Russian music come shining through Rachmaninov's two widely different works, the magnificent Second Piano Concerto and the virtuosic Rhapsody on a Theme of Paganini, both analysed in the* Listener's Guide, *Rachmaninov composed in the shadow of World War I; its effect on his contemporary artists and writers is described in* In The Background.

Sergei Rachmaninov was born in 1873 to an aristocratic family in Oneg, but his father squandered the family fortune; his parents separated, and Rachmaninov moved to St. Petersburg with his mother. He was awarded a scholarship to study at the Moscow Conservatoire in 1882, where his talent came to the attention of his cousin Alexander Siloti, a concert pianist. Siloti arranged for private lessons with Nikolay Zverev, whose stern discipline helped Rachmaninov to hone his virtuoso skills. Although his fame as both a composer and a concert pianist grew soon after he left the Conservatoire, he was self-critical and sensitive; a poor performance could cast him into deep depression. Between 1906 and 1910, a series of highly acclaimed works, a successful marriage and triumphant concert tours of the United States helped him to establish some personal eqilibrium. In later years his works went in and out of favour in Russia, but he lived an isolated life in California, where he died in 1943.

COMPOSER'S LIFE

# *'Last Romantic'*

**Sergei Rachmaninov, last of the great Russian Romantic composers, found himself out of step with his country's politics and music, yet he went on to produce some of this century's best-loved works.**

For Sergei Rachmaninov's music we are deeply indebted to his father, Vasily. A spendthrift, gambler and womanizer, he broke up the family home, squandered the family fortune and made young Sergei's early life insecure and unstable. Yet, in doing so, he undoubtedly diverted his son from what would have been his natural family vocation — a career as a professional soldier — and, instead, indirectly set him on a musical course.

Against this background of emotional upheaval, the young Sergei, sensitive, moody and unruly, grew and developed. Though hailed early on by his teachers for his prodigious musical talent he sometimes showed a lack of self-confidence in terms of his creative ability and frequently found himself out of step with the music of the time. Despite all this his work came to be admired as containing some of the finest examples of late-Romantic music.

*On leaving Russia in 1918 Rachmaninov believed that his future lay as a performer rather than as a composer. Indeed, his fame in his later years outside Russia rested on his career as a virtuoso pianist and recording artist. He is shown here at the Steinway piano given to him by the Steinway Company in America. During his first few months in America he gave nearly 40 concerts and recitals.*

Courtesy of Steinway and Sons/Photo by Christopher Barker

*Rachmaninov's parents: father, Vasily (top) and mother, Lubov (below). They separated in 1881.*

*After his parents' separation, Sergei's maternal grandmother played an active part in the boy's life. She bought an estate at Borivoso near the river Volkhov and it was here that Sergei spent his summer holidays swimming and canoeing in the countryside (right).*

## Family turmoil

Sergei was born into an aristocratic Russian family on 1 April 1873. His father, a handsome, dashing army officer had done well for himself in marrying a wealthy general's daughter – Lubov Butakova – and had inherited a dowry of five large country estates. Devoted to the pursuit of pleasure, Vasily could now afford to indulge himself further and he left the army to lead the life of a gentleman landowner. Unfortunately for Lubov he also continued to indulge his bachelor ways. By the time Sergei was nine only one of the estates remained in the family's possession – the others had been sold to pay for his father's lavish taste for expensive women and his gambling debts. Soon, even the last estate had to go too and the family – which now included five other children besides Sergei – were forced to take a flat in St Petersburg.

There was no question, now, of expensive education for the children – alternatives had to be found, and quickly, for at home Vasily's and Lubov's marriage was breaking down under the strain of their straitened circumstances. Divorce, however was neither socially nor religiously acceptable so, instead, they separated. Vasily left the flat to Lubov and the children.

In the meantime, Sergei, who had shown considerable ability on the piano, having been taught since the age of five, was lined up for a musical education. Consequently, in 1882 Sergei entered the St Petersburg Conservatory on a scholarship.

Unfortunately, Sergei was not the best of students, which is hardly surprising considering the disruptive effect of his family background on his sensitive nature. He did only a minimum of work and frequently played truant – roaming the streets with gangs of boys instead of studying. When his reports came out he altered them to deceive his mother.

*From the autumn of 1885 until the summer of 1892 Rachmaninov was a student at the Conservatory in Moscow (left). For the first four years in Moscow he lived under the strict regime of his tutor Zverev (seated, far right). Sergei (second from left) and a few other particularly gifted pupils lived at Zverev's home. With the help of his sister, Zverev supervised their education and saw that they were exposed to the finest musical talent in Moscow.*

One stabilizing influence on him, however, was his maternal grandmother. Every winter when she visited St Petersburg, she devoted a lot of time to him. After church on Sundays she encouraged him to play the music they had heard and rewarded him with twenty-five kopecks a performance. She also bought a country estate at Borivoso, near the river Volkhov, where Sergei spent his summer holidays.

By 1885, however, matters came to a head at the Conservatory. Sergei's musical education had to some extent been mismanaged, as his teachers were so impressed by his technique and perfect pitch that they overlooked weaknesses in basic theory. His laziness in general subjects, though, was so unforgivable that, in 1885, they threatened to withdraw his scholarship. His mother turned for advice to her nephew, Alexander Siloti, himself a brilliant pianist, who advised a course with his own former teacher, Nikolai Zverev, in Moscow.

Sergei, apprehensive as any twelve-year-old boy might be about leaving home and family for the first time, was worried by the stories he heard regarding Zverev's stern discipline and insistence on hard work.

### Studies in Moscow

The new régime was as strict as he had feared, but not unkind. Zverev, a distinguished teacher at the Moscow Conservatory, made a habit of taking a few particularly gifted pupils into his home where, with his sister's help, he supervised their whole education. His control over their lives was total — they were not even allowed home for the holidays — but no payment was expected and there were frequent free outings to theatres and concerts. At the weekends it was open house to the finest musical talents in Moscow. In this way the pupils met, and played for, such famous musicians as Anton Rubinstein, Glazunov and Tchaikovsky.

In the summer of 1886 Zverev took his protégés to the Crimea, where they stayed on the estate of a Moscow millionaire whose children Zverev was teaching. They were accompanied by a professor of theory and harmony from the Conservatory, whose task it was to prepare them for next year's studies. Rachmaninov seems to have found this exciting and stimulating, for it prompted his first attempts at composition. The following year he produced an arrangement for two pianos of Tchaikovsky's Manfred symphony, which won the great composer's approval, and also presented a set of nocturnes for piano to Zverev. But Zverev's ambitions for him were centred on playing rather than composing and this was a source of disagreement between them which finally, when Rachmaninov was sixteen, reached a dramatic climax. Rachmaninov went to Zverev and asked that he be allowed a room of his own in which to compose and practise, instead of sharing with his fellow pupils as he had done for the past three years. How tactfully this request was put we do not know, but Zverev seems to have thought him arrogant and ungrateful as a result.

Although Rachmaninov stayed at the Conservatory quarters for another month, the situation became impossible, as Zverev refused even to speak to him and eventually he moved into the house of some relatives, the Satins, who lived nearby. Initially this was embarrassing, since Rachmaninov had hardly visited them at all during his time in the city. Nevertheless he found them welcoming and kind and they offered him the sort of intimate family atmosphere he had not experienced for some time.

Fortunately, Zverev had ceased to teach Rachmaninov personally, so his studies at the Conservatory were not seriously affected by the rift. However, in the spring of 1891, Siloti, who had been teaching him piano for three years, resigned his post

64

С. РАХМАНИНОВ
SERGEI RACHMANINOV
OP.13

ПЕРВАЯ
СИМФОНИЯ
FIRST
SYMPHONY

ПАРТИТУРА
SCORE

ГОСУДАРСТВЕННОЕ МУЗЫКАЛЬНОЕ ИЗДАТЕЛЬСТВО
STATE   MUSIC   PUBLISHERS
МОСКВА ✦ MOSCOW ✦ ЛЕНИНГРАД ✦ LENINGRAD
1 9 4 7

*During the three years after the disastrous first performance in 1897 of his First Symphony (title page above) Rachmaninov found it impossible to compose. He spent his summers on the estate of relatives (left) and launched himself on a new career as an opera conductor with the Moscow Private Opera Company. Here he met and became a close friend of the singer Shalyapin (right).*

after a disagreement with the new director. Rachmaninov did not want to be taught by anyone else and applied, successfully, to take his final piano examination a year early. This gave him only three weeks to prepare the set pieces, but nevertheless he passed with honours. The following year, 1892, he surprised his examiners in composition even more. The students were required to compose a one-act opera, *Aleko,* based on a poem by Pushkin. Rachmaninov presented a fully orchestrated score within eighteen days and was awarded the Great Gold Medal, which had only been won twice previously in the history of the Conservatory. He was also reconciled with Zverev who, quite won over by the success of his former pupil, presented him with his gold watch in congratulation.

Rachmaninov had composed other works, including a piano concerto, during his last two years at the Conservatory and had also given his first public recital. On leaving the Conservatory he was introduced to the music publishers, Gutheil, who offered him five hundred roubles for a set of pieces including *Aleko.* Later that year he composed a *Prelude in C sharp minor for piano* which was to

become his most famous composition – he was obliged to play it, if only as an encore, at almost all his subsequent concerts. But he was not yet confident that he could earn a living from playing and composing, and for the next few years took on teaching work, which he heartily disliked. Then, about this time, his life entered another very disturbed and unsettled phase.

His stay with the Satins lasted only for a couple of years and he moved out, first to live with a fellow student and then for a while with his father, who had come to Moscow to work. He then rented a tiny furnished flat of his own for a few months, but by the end of 1894 he was back with the Satins, who offered him a bedroom and a studio in a new, larger house they had bought. He was upset by the deaths of Zverev and Tchaikovsky; the latter, who, despite the difference in their ages had been a real friend, and whose encouragement during his adolescent years had given him much confidence and security. Also at this time he developed an infatuation for a young married woman named Anna Lodizhensky. His feelings found expression in the restless and intense music of the *First Symphony,* which was dedicated to her.

*In 1902 Rachmaninov married his first cousin Natalia Satina (left). Her family home (above) at Ivanovka became the focal point of their happy lives for the next ten years.*

The first performance, in St Petersburg in March 1897, was under-rehearsed and badly performed, and Rachmaninov was so appalled by what he heard that he could not bear to sit in the concert hall. Next day, the St Petersburg critics, ever eager to attack a musician from the rival city of Moscow, savaged the work.

Rachmaninov was totally shattered by the rejection of a work into which he had put so much of himself, and composed nothing more for three years.

However, he was introduced to the millionaire industrialist Mamontov who ran the Moscow Private Opera Company and began another career, this time as a conductor for the company's 1897–8 season. He met the great singer Shalyapin who was to become a close friend for forty years. In the summer of 1898 he attended Shalyapin's marriage to the Italian ballerina Tornaghi. The bridal pair were serenaded at six the following morning by an improvised band playing household implements, conducted by Rachmaninov. Despite these diversions, on the whole, his mood was one of melancholy and his creativity was stifled.

**Confidence returns**

He made a visit to England in 1899, playing and conducting, and promised the London Philharmonic Society a new piano concerto, but he was unable to make any progress with it. In desperation, he consulted Dr Nikolay Dahl, a Moscow physician who specialized in treatment by hypnosis. The results were spectacularly successful; within a few months he had completed two movements of the new concerto, which were performed to an enthusiastic reception in Moscow in December, and in 1900 the finished concerto, the *Second Piano Concerto* was published and dedicated to Dahl.

As proof of confidence in him, Rachmaninov's cousin Siloti offered him a substantial loan, to be repaid over the next three years. With renewed confidence in his financial security and powers of composition, he asked his cousin Natalia Satina to marry him. Since marriage between first cousins was frowned upon by the Orthodox church, special permission of the Tsar had to be obtained. Eventually the wedding took place on 29 April 1902.

The next ten years or so were ostensibly the most successful of Rachmaninov's life, with his career advancing on all fronts and a happy marriage soon made happier by the births of two daughters.

During the decade he spent two seasons as

*Rachmaninov's period of lack of creativity was alleviated by treatment from a hypnotist, Dr Nikolay Dahl, and by his marriage. His return to successful composing was marked by the **Second Concerto**. However, although now highly regarded as a composer, he was still plagued by self-doubt. One unwavering drive, though, was his religion – Russian Orthodoxy. He composed two major religious works and in these and many of his other compositions can be heard music reminiscent of the great bells of the cathedral in the town of Novgorod (below) – the sight and sound of which were very familiar to him.*

conductor of Moscow's Imperial opera. He travelled extensively, making his first trip to America in 1909, and then spending three successive winters in Dresden. He gave many concerts and recitals and composed much of his finest music, including the *Second Symphony*, the *Third Piano Concerto*, the symphonic poem *'The Isle of the Dead'*, inspired by a picture by the Swiss artist Böcklin, and his choral symphony *The Bells*, based on a poem by Edgar Allan Poe. From 1910–1912 he was also vice-President of the Imperial Russian Music Society.

The pursuit of so many different activities imposed a heavy strain on his health, and he particularly resented the limits set upon his time for composition. He suffered severe pains in his head and back, and in his letters to friends constantly complained of ill-health and general tiredness, almost to the point of hypochondria. And in spite of his conspicuous success, he still remained a victim of his own self-doubt.

One unwavering consolation to him seems to have been his religion. Even from his childhood the services and especially the music of the Orthodox church had a deep effect on him. He composed two major religious works for unaccompanied choir, *The Liturgy of St John Chrysostom* and the *Vesper Mass*.

### Into exile

As Rachmaninov moved into middle age, Russia became an increasingly turbulent place, with war outside its borders and revolution threatening within. He seems to have had uncertain feelings about the new political ideas which threatened the old régime. As early as 1905 he added his name to a

declaration which stated that 'There is but one way out of this impasse: Russia must at long last enter the path of basic reforms'. And yet, as an aristocrat and landowner, he stood to lose most from these reforms. The hostile attitude of the peasants to him when he visited the Ivanovka estate in the spring of 1917 finally convinced him that things would never be the same again. As the year proceeded and the actions of government and governed became more extreme, he desperately sought some means of escape for himself and his family, even if on a temporary basis. The opportunity of a concert tour of Sweden presented itself in November 1917 and Rachmaninov snatched the chance; he obtained the necessary passes for his wife and children, and they crossed the Finnish frontier on 23 December, clutching a minimum of possessions and a gift of bread and caviar from Shalyapin. He was never to set foot in Russia again.

Although still only in his mid-forties, Rachmaninov had already composed 39 of his eventual 45 published works when he began his self-imposed exile. His main consideration was now to earn money and he realized that his best chance of doing this was as conductor and piano virtuoso.

After a few months in Stockholm and Copenhagen the Rachmaninovs moved to the United States of America where Sergei felt he would be more secure financially. His first few months there – he arrived in November 1918 – were spent giving concerts and making recordings. Although New York was to be his base for many years he kept his interests in Europe.

In the spring of 1926, just before the birth of his

first grandchild, Sergei and his wife had a family reunion in France with their daughters. Tragedy marred the event: his daughter Irina's husband, Prince Volkonsky died suddenly.

With the intention of helping his widowed daughter Rachmaninov set up a publishing house – TAIR, – which was to publish works by Russian émigré composers. The company was run by his two daughters.

From 1926 he spent more time in Europe. For a number of years he rented a villa in Clairfontaine, a village about an hour's drive from Paris, and there held court in the old Russian style. Russian-speaking company was not hard to find, as there were many exiles in Europe, including members of both the Siloti and the Satin families.

In 1930 he purchased some land beside Lake Lucerne and built a villa there which he named Senar. Although he loved its peace and seclusion, and also enjoyed trips across the lake in his new motor boat, he still travelled regularly to play and conduct, and continued to make historic recordings for the Victor Record Company. He would have nothing to do with radio broadcasting though, insisting stubbornly, though at the time perhaps correctly, that the sound quality was too poor to do justice to the music. He always preferred to play to a live audience.

In 1931 Rachmaninov put his name to an anti-Soviet manifesto published in the New York Times, and the Soviet government responded by banning performances of all his music in Russia. *Pravda* described him contemptuously as 'a composer who was played out long ago and whose music is that of an insignificant imitator and reactionary'. An overstatement, naturally, but not without a grain of truth; even while he still lived in Russia, his music was regarded condescendingly by the avant-garde, and Rachmaninov confessed himself quite out of sympathy with the trends in the twentieth century music represented by Prokofiev and Stravinsky. Nonetheless, he continued to compose – the *Third Symphony,* the *Rhapsody on a theme of Paganini* and the *Symphonic Dances* all date from the last decade of his life and prove that he still had a

*Because of the turbulent political situation in Russia in 1918 Rachmaninov (left) and his family decided to leave Russia. They moved first to Stockholm and Copenhagen, but eventually decided to settle in America. He arrived in New York (above) in November 1918 and although he lived from time to time in parts of Europe, America became his home until his death in 1943.*

distinctive, if unfashionable, voice.

As old age approached, so did more upheavals. In 1938 he lost his dear friend Shalyapin; he visited him twice a day as he lay in hospital in Paris, and was greatly shocked by his death. By the next year it was clear that there would be another war in Europe, and the house on Lake Lucerne, Senar, had to be abandoned. Rachmaninov sailed back to the United States in August 1939, accompanied by his wife, his elder daughter Irina and grandaughter Sophia.

Once back in America, he threw himself into his work, but it was impossible to forget the situation in Europe. His younger daughter Tatiana, her husband and their son Alexander, remained in France and news of them was almost impossible to obtain. The German invasion of Russia caused him great sadness though by donating the proceeds of many of his concerts to the Fund for Russian War Relief, he found himself in favour again with the Soviet government.

Early in 1943, he had to abandon a concert tour because of a sudden deterioration in his health and on 28 March 1943 he died of cancer in California. The funeral was held in Beverley Hills, but his remains were later taken to Kensico in New York State, where he lies buried in a quiet cemetery attached to a Russian orthodox church.

# Orchestral works

*The rich melodies and dazzling piano displays of the Piano Concerto No. 2 and the 'Paganini Rhapsody' show Rachmaninov at his best and they are deservedly popular and widely loved.*

## Piano Concerto No. 2

Rachmaninov's beautiful *Second Piano Concerto* is dedicated, remarkably, to his psychiatrist Dr Nikolay Dahl – few dedications have been so well merited.

In 1897, three years before writing the concerto, the young composer had been thrown into terrible depression by the hammering his first symphony had received at the hands of the critics. It seemed he would never have the confidence to compose again. Then in spring 1900, his aunt sent him to Dr Dahl.

Within a few months he was composing again with such speed and sureness of touch that he had completed the second and third movements of a new concerto, his second for piano, by the end of August. Before the end of the year, the concerto (minus the first movement) had been premièred in Moscow to tremendous critical acclaim. Several of the critics expressed keen interest in how Rachmaninov would complete the concerto.

The first movement was written early in 1901, and the première of the complete concerto took place at a Moscow Philharmonic Society Concert on 9th November. The reception was rapturous. The new movement surpassed everyone's expectations and the work as a whole was welcomed as a major addition to the repertory.

## Programme notes

The popularity of the second piano concerto has continued to grow over the years. Audiences everywhere have warmed to the brilliance, colour and abundant lyricism of this magnificent work. Today, more than 80 years after that triumphant première, it has become one of the best-loved concertos of all time.

### First movement: Moderato

The concerto opens in a strikingly original way with eight bars of sonorous, bell-like chords of the piano. This chiming figure sets the mood for the movement.

The sound of bells meant a great deal to Rachmaninov. As a child he had been deeply impressed by the chimes of St Sophia's Cathedral, Novgorod, and in later life he frequently expressed the view that bells

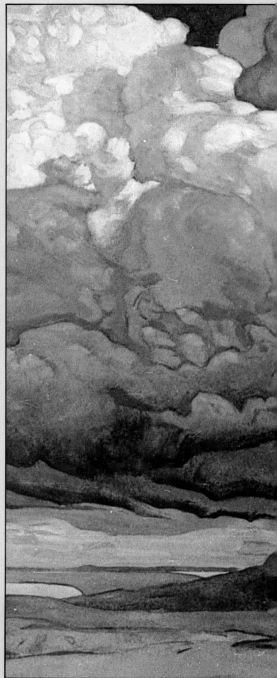

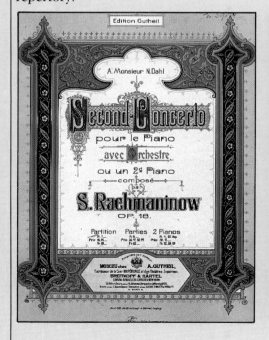

*The title page of the Piano Concerto No 2 (far left) shows the dedication to Dr Nikolay Dahl, the psychiatrist who gave Rachmaninov the confidence to write the work.*

*The ominous chiming chords that open the concerto may have been inspired by the tolling of the bells of St Sophia's Cathedral in Novgorod (characterized left).*

could suggest a variety of human emotions. Here the mood is dark and tragic.

Soon the strings glide in over the piano to develop the mood with a sombre and passionate theme in a minor key. Typically Russian, Rachmaninov makes the most of this rich melody and allows it to unfold

*Like so much Russian music, Rachmaninov's piano concerto has a brooding expansiveness that seems to echo the vast open spaces of the Russian landscape. Rich melodies are not dropped once they have done their job, in the Western style, but are allowed to unfold gradually, like great grey storm clouds tumbling through the sky (left).*

gradually over another 29 bars. At first, the soloist lingers in the background, embellishing the harmonies with cascading *arpeggios.* But the piano soon comes quietly to the fore, pushing the tempo, until the melody explodes into a vigorous climax. At the last moment, the orchestra turns suddenly from C minor to E flat major and the mood brightens considerably. A short but highly expressive figure on violas leads into a beautiful singing, piano solo.

Example 2

Again, the melody unravels gradually before the tempo quickens and the piano's quicksilver figurations bring the section to a close.

A series of grimly powerful brass chords, marked *pesante* (heavy) bring the music firmly back to the original C minor and a dramatic development ensues. This begins edgily with the first melody on violas, *mezzo forte* (moderately loud). An ominous rhythmic figure on cellos and basses winds up the tension with an echo of the bell motif. Then the soloist takes command, again pushing the pace with a series of dazzling runs. Finally, the second melody (Example 2) reappears on violas, but its character has changed drastically;

*The stormy turbulence (left) of the 'maestoso alla marcia' gathers to a powerful climax, creating one of the highlights of the concerto's first movement.*

now it seems fearful and imploring. As the violins enter the fray, it rises to an impassioned climax, decorated by massive triplets from the soloist.

A feverishly excited bridge passage leads into the stormy recapitulation, marked *Maestoso, alla marcia* (majestic, march-like). The sombre first melody returns *fortissimo* on violins, violas and cellos, while the piano thunders out the rhythmic quaver figure of the bell motif.

The tension subsides and the piano drifts along sadly, but just as the music seems about to come wearily to rest in C minor, the harmony changes magically to A flat major. The horn quietly presents the second melody (Example 2) above shimmering strings and, for the moment, all is peace. The sense of relief is short-lived, however, for the music slips back into C minor. Piano and orchestra ponder sadly on what might have been, before an almost brutally concise coda leads the movement to an end in an angry shout on strings and piano.

**Second movement: Adagio sostenuto**
Like the opening movement, the *adagio* begins with a short chordal introduction, but here warm and soothing strings, subtly coloured by low woodwind and horns, lift the music gently from the gloomy C minor to a radiant E major. The piano enters with a series of rippling *legato* (smooth) triplets above which flute and clarinet sing a haunting theme.

Example 3

A few years earlier, Rachmaninov had included some lines from Byron's *Parisina* in the score of his Suite no 1 for two pianos; these words seem to encapsulate the mood at the opening of the *adagio*.

*It is the hour when from the boughs*
*The nightingale's high note is heard;*
*It is the hour when lovers' vows*
*Seem sweet in every whispered word;*
*And gentle winds and waters near,*
*Make music to the lonely ear.*

The piano takes up this limpid theme before a brief but heartfelt climax brings the music quietly on into the more impassioned middle section of the movement. If the opening theme created an image of 'gentle winds, and waters near', here the piano ardently expresses the more personal feelings of the lonely poet. Tension mounts as the tempo increases and a brilliant, powerful piano *cadenza* (solo) climaxes with three massive chords. But, just when it seems the earlier serenity has been lost for ever, two low flutes enter, *pianissimo* (very softly), and the music resumes its original calm. It is as though in the midst of all those impassioned keyboard pyrotechnics some gentle voice has whispered 'hush'. Muted violins and then solo piano lead the movement to a beautiful, warm close.

**Third movement: Allegro scherzando**
The finale begins martially with a jerky rhythmic figure on strings, low woodwind and tuba. But after only six bars the music turns abruptly to C major. There is a thrill-

*The fragile beauty of the adagio's opening when 'gentle winds, and waters near, make music to the lonely ear,' soon gives way to the impassioned revery of the 'lonely ear' – the solitary poet wandering in the garden (below).*

*Some way through the allegro, as the glorious second subject runs its course, a mysterious stillness comes over the music and the pace drops to a slow, funeral march (left).*

ing *crescendo* and the soloist returns to the fray with a brief but dramatic solo passage. A few bars of nervous dialogue between piano and woodwind usher in an unusually terse theme, based on a repeated rhythmic pattern. For a while the martial elements seem in command of the music, but this display of musical 'machismo' fades to prepare the way for the second subject.

The soloist dwells expansively on this melody before something extraordinary happens; a mysterious stillness comes over the music and a much slower version of the martial first theme is heard on *pizzicato* (plucked) strings and woodwind, decorated by piano triplets and coloured by quietly clashed cymbals.

A sudden surge from solo piano launches a development led by breathtakingly brilliant piano passages. A dazzling climax is reached, then the second subject returns, richly and warmly scored. A ghostly reminder of the opening of the development is banished by brighter harmonies before an exultant cadenza introduces Rachmaninov's most dramatic surprise: the victorious return of the second subject on full orchestra and piano.

No sooner has this great tune finished than the piano breaks out into joyous helter-skelter figurations accompanied by loud acclamations from the orchestra. With these triumphant sounds, the young composer celebrates the long-awaited return of his muse. 'Rejoice with me' he seems to say. The invitation is irresistible.

## Rhapsody on a theme of Paganini

Rachmaninov wrote relatively little music

*The Debut of Paganini*
*Harmonics a Sol Corde*
*Sketched at Opera House*

*Niccolo Paganini (left), the great violin virtuoso, was rumoured to have gained his talent by selling his soul to the devil – Rachmaninov's 'Paganini Rhapsody', based on a theme from the virtuoso's 'Caprice', is certainly full of demonic wit and virtuosity.*

after he left Russia in 1917. Indeed, with the exception of the *Fourth Piano Concerto* he composed virtually nothing for 14 years. Then in 1931 he wrote a set of variations on a theme by the Italian composer Arcangelo Corelli (1653-1713). Despite dispiriting receptions, Rachmaninov was highly pleased with the Corelli variations and he began to write a set of variations for piano and orchestra based on the famous A minor *Caprice* for solo violin by the great violin virtuoso, Niccolo Paganini.

This simple but curiously memorable idea had been used before by many other major composers – Brahms and Liszt are perhaps the most notable examples – but Rachmaninov obviously felt that there was much more that could be done with it. The theme provides considerable scope for variation. But there were other reasons why Paganini's theme might have appealed to Rachmaninov.

By the end of the 19th century, Paganini had come to symbolize the glamorous romantic virtuoso. There is an element of the fantastic in the Paganini legend. For a long time after his death it was rumoured that the great violinist had sold his soul to the devil in exchange for his phenomenal talents – Russian artists have always been drawn to supernatural subjects and more than any other mature work of Rachmaninov, the Rhapsody is full of bizarre colours and demonic humour.

## Programme notes

Although the Rhapsody is in one continuous movement, Rachmaninov has ingeniously divided the music into four distinct sections resembling the traditional

*The baleful plainsong Dies Irae, interwoven with Paganini's theme in the seventh variation, is an ancient liturgical chant telling of the terrors of the Day of Judgement (left), and it is one of Rachmaninov's favourite chants.*

four movements of a symphony. The first eleven variations are all in the same key – A minor – and all but two of these (the seventh and the eleventh) keep to the original tempo – *allegro vivace*. This gives variations 1-10 something of the character of a fast first movement.

The opening is boldly unconventional. Nine brusque bars of introduction lead to the first variation. This is based on the bare bones of Paganini's theme, stripped, as it were, of its melodic 'flesh'. This skeletal effect is enhanced by the scoring which is dominated by the sharp dry sounds of *staccato* brass and percussion.

Only when Variation 1 has run its course does the theme itself appear on violins, while piano picks out the thematic skeleton. In Variation 2 the piano takes up the theme, adding grotesque 'snaps' and a few piquant harmonies, while horns and trumpets provide the skeleton. In Variation 3 the theme begins to fragment. Violins and woodwind chatter to one another in repeated semiquavers while the piano tries to soften some of the rough edges with a sequence of short legato phrases. The soloist comes to the fore again in Variation 4 before the violins change the mood with short eery sighs. Variation 5 is wickedly funny. The piano part is dominated by rapid alternations between the two hands and sudden swift upward rushes. No matter how polished or refined the performance, the listener is irresistibly reminded of the keyboard acrobatics of that great entertainer, Chico Marx. In Variation 6 the piano seems to wander away abstractedly at the end of each phrase, but the beautiful, dream-like atmosphere is soon shattered.

Variation 7 introduces a new theme, a baleful plainsong melody *Dies Irae* (Day of Wrath) which depicts the terrors of the last judgement.

The powerful, sonorous piano writing in Variation 8 is reminiscent of Brahms, but the quick-fire exchanges between piano and orchestra are pure Rachmaninov. In the weird-sounding Variation 9 wood-wind, side-drum and strings patter out an exciting triplet rhythm while the soloist adds off-beat chords. In Variation 10, the *Dies Irae* lumbers in again on piano but trumpets and trombones seize upon the melody and give it a jazz-like syncopated rhythm.

The tempo drops to *moderato* for Variation 11. This is, in effect, an accompanied cadenza. The soloist seems to be trying to extend the theme lyrically, but the chilling string tremors seem to intimidate him. The piano writing dissolves into quiet, harp-like passages and the variation ends with a whispered reference to Paganini's theme.

Variations 12-15 form a kind of minuet-scherzo movement. Variation 12 is a slow, melancholy dance while Variation 13 is also dance-like, but the dancing becomes much more energetic. Paganini's theme is clearly audible in the strings and the piano adds heavy chords on the second and third beats of each bar. A sudden shift to F major marks the opening of the vigorous Variation 14. In Variation 15 the tempo increases still further.

The next three variations constitute the 'slow movement' of the piece. Variations 16 and 17 are mostly in the dark key of B flat minor, but, at the end of Variation 17 the key changes to D flat major and the piano writing is suddenly suffused with warmth. The next variation (18) is without doubt the most beautiful. It features one of the finest of Rachmaninov's 'big tunes' — yet the opening phrase is actually nothing more than Paganini's theme upside down! Strings take the theme to a radiant climax but eventually the piano is left to linger affectionately over the opening phrase of this wonderful melody.

Six bars of plangent *pizzicato* string chords bring about an abrupt transition to the original A minor and the piano sets off at a brisk tempo. The last six variations are so skilfully dovetailed that it isn't always easy to tell where one begins and another ends. Far better to approach Variations 19-24 as an exhilarating finale. The soloist leads the orchestra in a wild dance culminating in a terrifying climax at Variation 22. The *Dies Irae* returns thrillingly on piano and there is a sudden dislocating change of harmony to E flat. The soloist tears about distractedly as though seeking an exit from the prevailing A minor. A harmonic tug-of-war ensues between piano and orchestra, the former trying vainly to play through Paganini's theme in A flat minor, the latter insisting on A minor. It is the orchestra that wins, and in Variation 23 the theme returns in its original form on full orchestra.

Variation 24 is really the coda of the work, and it gives both soloist and orchestra the opportunity for an unparalleled display of brilliance. The *Dies Irae* returns portentously on brass and strings, but it too is caught up in the dance. The music thunders towards its conclusion; but Rachmaninov has one last trick left up his sleeve. At the last moment, the final two bars of Paganini's theme return quietly on piano with a bare *pizzicato* string accompaniment. It is a devastatingly simple ending. The effect is rather like someone snuffing out a candle, after which we are left in darkness.

## Understanding music: 20th-century pianism

The role of the piano in music — pianism — has been the focus of much attention in the 20th century. During this time many composers have sought to re-examine the piano's capabilities and traditional role as it has been previously understood by the great Romantics.

20th-century pianism basically starts with the innovations of Claude Debussy. The *Preludes* and *Images,* in particular, are full of beautiful and arresting effects: blending of chords by the subtle use of the pedal, exploitation of sympathetic vibrations (strings set in motion by the harmonics of lower notes of chords) and the treatment of individual chords as sonorities in their own right rather than as stages in a larger harmonic process.

Inspired by Debussy's innovations, other composers began to experiment with the piano, though not necessarily following Debussy's lines. The publisher Durand once remarked 'You forgot that the piano had hammers when Debussy

*The lovely 18th variation is a stroke of genius — Rachmaninov turns Paganini's theme upside down to create a romantic melody echoed in the beauty of the sublime face (left).*

played', yet Stravinsky, though a fervent admirer of Debussy, looked at the piano quite differently: 'If a piano has hammers, why try to alter its nature?' Consequently, Stravinsky used the piano essentially as a percussion instrument and his piano music is generally dry and almost wilfully inexpressive. This percussive style had many imitators, notably, Stravinsky's compatriot, Prokofiev and the Polish composer, Karol Szymanowski (1882–1937). In his mature piano works, however, Szymanowski balances his more experimental writing with an appealing, almost Chopinesque lyricism. Bartók, too, delighted in percussive effects; in his hands the piano often sounds more like a xylophone or a celesta. His famous collection of studies, *Mikrokosmos,* is prized by piano students for its unceasing inventiveness and originality.

The repertory of unusual effects has continued to grow over the century. The American, Henry Cowell (1897–1965), pioneered the use of the 'tone cluster' (the pianist is required to strike a group of notes with the hand); while more recently,

composers such as John Cage have written works for a 'prepared piano', in which objects are placed on or between the piano strings in order to change the tone quality of the instrument. Other modern scores demand the strings to be struck with fingers or with wooden or metal hammers. An introductory note in the score of Robert Sherlaw Johnson's second piano sonata lists nearly twenty different ways of playing inside the piano!

Piano teaching methods, as well as composers, also had an effect on 20th-century pianism, after specialist teachers emerged in the late 19th century. The most influential of these was Theodor Leschetizky (1850–1915). Among his many pupils were Paderewski, Benno Moiseiwitsch and Artur Schnabel. Unlike many of the conservatory teachers of his day, Leschetizky underplayed the need for technical mastery of the instrumental in favour of a practical approach to the music. And after Leschetizky fewer teachers were content to rely on prescribed methods.

Teachers and composers aside, many

pianists have played a part in developing pianism in this century via their brilliant interpretive approach to new piano music. The German, Walter Gieseking (1895–1956) devoted much of his time to championing the piano works of Schoenberg, Szymanowsky, Hindemith and the great Italian pianist-composer Busoni, but he is chiefly remembered for his masterly interpretations of the French masters, Debussy and Ravel (held by many to be the finest on record). The Rumanian, Dinu Lipatti (1917–1950) and the Russian-born Vladimir Horowitz (b. 1904) also included 20th-century works in their programmes.

In more recent times the brilliant Italian virtuoso, Maurizio Pollini has produced a number of highly acclaimed recordings of modern piano compositions, including the notorious second piano sonata of Pierre Boulez, a work that was once considered unplayable.

Nevertheless, despite the innovations of 20th-century pianism it is the piano music of the Classical and Romantic composers that has remained as the ultimate challenge for instrument and artist.

## *Great interpreters*

Decca International

Decca International

### Sir Adrian Boult (conductor)

Born in Chester in 1889, Sir Adrian's recorded legacy is vast, stretching as it does from 1920 till shortly before his death in 1983. Apart from covering an enormous range, he also re-recorded particular favourites as technology advanced –*The Planets* he recorded four times – and he became universally respected as a conductor of Handel and Brahms, as well as being perhaps the definitive interpreter of Elgar and Vaughan-Williams. An undemonstrative conductor, he wielded his undeniable authority through his marvellous sense of musical structure, his instinct for the 'right' tempo and a superb ear for orchestral balance and colour. He is indisputably one of this century's great conductors.
*Sir Adrian Boult (top)
and Julius Katchen*

### Julius Katchen (pianist)

Katchen was born in New Jersey, USA, in 1926. Aged 11, he had made his musical debut playing Schumann on a nationwide radio broadcast. Following this success, he was immediately engaged as a pianist by both the Philadelphia Philharmonic and by the New York Philharmonic, and appeared with these orchestras to great acclaim. Within a few years he had played all over Europe and by the mid-1950s, Katchen had moved permanently to Paris. Katchen had a large repertoire, although he specialized in Slavonic music and had a particular affinity with Gershwin's music, and his acknowledged intellectual power and great interpretative qualities made him an outstanding exponent of both Beethoven and Brahms. His untimely death in 1969 robbed the world of one of the great post-war pianists.

### FURTHER LISTENING

**Symphony No. 2 in E Minor**
This work abounds in characteristically rich melody, and the first movement is charged with an intense melancholy which is only relieved by powerful chords introducing the main theme. This use of strong contrasts runs through the whole work, where the scherzo movement is followed by a yearning largo third movement. Only in the finale are all the elements triumphantly unified into a positive and optimistic statement. This happy unity has helped it retain its popularity.

**The Isle of the Dead**
Inspired by Arnold Böcklin's painting of the same name, this orchestral 'tone poem' is

easily one of the composer's most impressive achievements. The mood of the picture, with its boat slowly coming ashore, is eerily and uncannily heightened in the music as the rhythmic rowing and the lapping waters are heard throughout the orchestra. Various ghostly images hover in the mind before the last wrenching climax.

**Symphonic Dances, op. 45**
These pieces, redolent with the air of his homeland, were Rachmaninov's swansong. The music is written to illustrate certain dance rhythms, rather than to be actually danced to. They show brilliant orchestration and contain some memorable melodies.

# IN THE BACKGROUND
# *'Call to arms'*

***In their paintings, poems and novels, a generation of artists inspired by World War I, the 'Great War', of 1914-18, reflected the full horror and tragedy of the conflict.***

As the early August sun sank behind the trees in London's St James's Park, in 1914, Sir Edward Grey, the British Foreign Secretary, stood thoughtfully at a window in the Foreign Office. Earlier that afternoon, he had almost wept as he saw 'the efforts of a lifetime go for nothing', and confessed, 'I feel like a man who has wasted his life'. Now all he could do was wait — wait for the German reply to Britain's ultimatum, a reply that might save the two countries from war. He knew it would not come. Germany's mobilization had gone too far. Then, as the sun finally dipped out of sight and the

golden glow vanished from the room, he said quietly, 'The lamps are going out all over Europe; we shall not see them lit again in our lifetime'.

His plaintive comment has echoed down the years. For, with Britain's entry into a conflict that had already ensnared Russia, Austria-Hungary, Serbia, Germany, Belgium and France, Europe was plunged into the most terrible war the world had ever known. Over 10 million men and women were killed, more than 20 million seriously wounded; five million women were widowed, nine million children orphaned and 10 million people made refugees.

***When war was declared, crowds thronged the streets, greeting the news with jubilation (right). Soon, though, the same young men were stumbling through a mire of horrors, having lost all sight of the war's purpose. Gassed (below) preserves the nightmare of battle.***

Yet Sir Edward Grey and a few fellow statesmen were terrifyingly alone in their response to the outbreak of war. Over much of Europe, the great majority greeted the news not with despair but euphoria. In Germany, on the night of 31st July, thousands of people had thronged the streets of Berlin, awaiting Russia's reply to the German ultimatum. All next day they waited, crowding round the Foreign Office in Wilhelmstrasse and the Royal Palace. Then, at 5.30 pm, a policeman came to the palace gates and announced that mobilization had been ordered. Germany was at war. As the news passed from mouth to mouth, the crowds erupted in boisterous cheering and burst into a spontaneous chorus of *Now thank we all our God*.

It was the same in Britain on the night of 4th August. Men and women dressed in light summer clothes packed Parliament Square and the Mall, shoulder to shoulder in the warm evening air. When the declaration of war was announced, they began to cheer wildly and sing *Land of hope and glory* and, like the people in Berlin, went off into the night, still singing, to celebrate until the early hours. Similar scenes were witnessed all over Europe. War fever was in the air.

**'Call to arms'**
Thousands of British, young and old, answered Kitchener's 'Call to Arms' and rushed to enlist. Recruitment was entirely voluntary at first, but

throughout autumn and the following spring, an endless stream of volunteers waited patiently in queues, sometimes two miles long. On a single day in September 1914, 30,000 men joined up and, in the three months after the outbreak of war, no less than 700,000 volunteered. Many thousands more had arrived only to be turned down on grounds of ill-health or age. Britain did not need to introduce conscription until January 1916, by which time over four million men had offered themselves for service.

The will to fight was common to all classes. Most remarkably, it was prevalent among artists, intellectuals and socialists. Men and women who had been internationalists and revolutionaries were transformed overnight into ardent patriots willing to support their country's war effort to the death. The thriving political organization, the Socialist International, was pledged to oppose war. Suddenly it crumbled, as thousands of erstwhile revolutionaries all over Europe abandoned their cause. The Russian revolutionary Georgi Plekhanov, in exile in France, actually became a recruiting agent for the French army, recruiting men to fight against former socialist comrades conscripted into the German army. The Social Democrat party in the German Reichstag (the party founded by Marx and Engels) voted unanimously for the introduction of war credits. Lenin was so astounded when he heard this news that he convinced himself the newspapers containing the reports were forgeries.

### Artistic idealists

In Britain, so many artists joined up that a batallion called the Artists' Rifles was formed. Painters such as John and Paul Nash and Charles Sergeant Jagger all saw active service in the Artists' Rifles. In his book, *Tommy goes to War,* Malcolm Brown quotes one artist's memories of the day after Britain joined the war:

*Would they* (the Germans) *invade us, I wondered. By George! If they should they'd find us a tougher nut to crack than they expected. My bosom swelled and I clenched my fist. I wished to do something desperate for the cause of England.*

Some were so keen to enlist that they lied about their age. The actor F. R. Benson gave his age as 34 – he was actually 56. 'Surely you're older than that?' asked the recruiting officer. 'Are you here to get soldiers or to ask silly questions?' Benson replied haughtily. He was turned down, but contributed to the war effort by giving performances of Shakespeare's patriotic *Henry V.* The royal portraitist John Lavery, then 58, was actually accepted into the Artist' Rifles, but the rigours of training proved too much:

*... the second or third route march did for me. I had to call in the doctor whose verdict was, 'My dear sir, go back to your paint pots; you will do more for your country with your brush than with your rifle' ... In the end, they went to the trenches and I went to bed.*

Others did join up, from the painter Wyndham Lewis to the composer Vaughan Williams, while many *did* contribute to the war effort 'with their brushes'. Alfred Leete's famous poster showing Kitchener pointing out and saying, 'Your Country Needs You!' is believed to have encouraged many thousands of men to enlist. Another brilliant poster painter, Frank Brangwyn had his services rejected.

The Parliamentary Recruiting Committee turned Brangwyn down, even when he offered to work for nothing. They felt Brangwyn's work was too complex – and too realistic – to have the desired effect.

Of course, there were artists who dissented from this war mania from the start. Prominent among these were members of the 'Bloomsbury set', the fashionable circle of artists and writers who used to meet at the Bloomsbury house of Lady Ottoline Morrell. Lytton Strachey and Bertrand Russell, both

*Both Germany and Britain chose the image of George and the Dragon (right) to symbolize the righteousness of their cause and to claim God for an ally. This heroic style of image was in keeping with the 'glamorous' image of war that prevailed in 1914. The poem of the moment ran:*
**Thou careless, awake! Thou peacemaker, fight! Stand England for honour, And God guard the Right!**

members of the set, suffered for their pacifist views. Russell was fined for 'statements likely to prejudice the recruiting and discipline of His Majesty's forces'.

Playwright George Bernard Shaw condemned the war and the rabid patriotism sweeping the country. He wrote an article in the *New Statesman* suggesting that the best way to end the war was for the troops to shoot all the officers and go home. H. G. Wells dismissed Shaw as 'an idiot child screaming in hospital'.

Those artists who went off to the Front did so for a variety of reasons. Some sought the emotional stimulus for their work. 'You must not miss a war . . . You cannot afford to miss that experience,' wrote Wyndham Lewis. Some went because they were curious. Others went out of sheer bravado. But the predominant mood was of quiet idealism and partriotism.

## The long, long trail to war

For 20 years, the fires of militarism had been fanned so ardently that the start of the war was almost a relief. Germany and England had been indulging in a race for naval superiority. In France, the concept of *revanchism* (revenge for their loss of Alsace and Lorraine to Germany in 1871), was so powerful that in 1913 compulsory military service was increased from two to three years by public demand. Young French people were taught in school that Germans were inferior and that Alsace and Lorraine had been cruelly wrenched away.

In Germany, patriotic, militarist pressure-groups advocated a build-up of arms. Like *revanchism* in France, these groups had considerable support among the young. In 1911, General von der Goltz had set up the *Jungdeutschlandbund* (Young Germans) to promote nationalist militarism among youth. The *Jungdeutschlandbund* glorified war. They said that when war came, as it inevitably would,

*it wil be more beautiful and wonderful to live forever among the heroes on a war memorial in a church than to die an empty death in bed, nameless . . . let that be heaven for young Germany.*

The Boy Scout movement in Britain, despite its peaceable nature nowadays, was very similar. The Boy Scout motto, 'Be Prepared', is actually a shortened version of Baden-Powell's exhortation to 'Be prepared to die for your country . . . so that when the time comes you may charge home with confidence, not caring whether you are to be killed or not!'

This was the kind of 'clean, healthy patriotism' that men like the poet Rupert Brooke carried into the

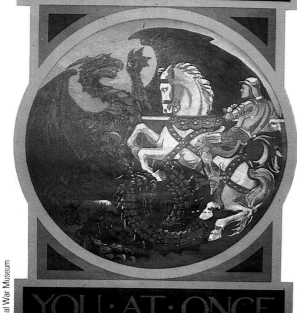

*German* **Uhlans** *(below left) – lancers reputed to ride down their enemies and die with a laugh – were the pride of the cavalry in 1914. But both cavalry and chivalry quickly disappeared in the mud and squalor of mechanized trench warfare, where the vast majority of soldiers were not professional but unskilled amateurs.*

*Artist John Nash grew all too familiar with 'Going over the Top' (below) and painted from experience.*

*John Nash's brother, Paul (above), was an official war artist, perhaps best remembered for his picture, The Menin Road. He and his brother both volunteered, and served in the battalion designated 'The Artists' Rifles'.*

war. His famous sonnet, *The Soldier,* reflects the dangerous innocence of it all:

> *If I should die, think only this of me;*
> *That there's some corner of a foreign field*
> *That is forever England . . .*

The British public had been fed German invasion stories in popular fiction such as William le Queux's *The Invasion of 1910,* serialized in 1906 in *The Daily Mail* (then the most popular daily newspaper in the country), and Erskine Childers' *The Riddle of the Sands* (1903). Le Queux's story in particular so caught the public imagination that many people felt cheated when 1910 came and the war had not started.

### The great escape

For some, war was a substitute for disappointed revolutionary hopes, removing men from a divided, unjust society to a community where all men were equal and shared a common fate.

Men like Robert Graves and T. E. Lawrence ('of Arabia'), jaded, disenchanted, middle-class sons saw in the army an escape from boredom, and a new purpose in life. The army would be 'real living'. In Germany, in particular, going off to war was seen as an escape from the industrial, urban society. Much art from the early war period has a distinctly pastoral flavour – almost as if war was a return to a healthy, open-air life. One of the most famous poems of the early months of the war is Julian Grenfell's *Into Battle,* published in *The Times* in May 1915. In this, battle is associated with natural images:

> *The naked earth is warm with Spring*
> *And with green grass and bursting trees*
> *Leans to the sun's gaze glorying*
> *And quivers in the sunny breeze;*
> *And life is colour and warmth and light,*
> *And a striving ever more for these;*
> *And he is dead who will not fight;*
> *And who dies fighting has increase . . .*

For millions of working men, going to war was to be an exciting break from the daily grind of work and poverty. The unemployed suddenly found a purpose in life.

### The course of the war

Most expected the war to last a matter of months. 'It will all be over by Christmas,' they said. But they were terribly wrong.

The war began when two million German troops began to sweep westwards towards France. They advanced rapidly along a vast front stretching from the foothills of the Alps right into Belgium. (It was the fact that they marched through 'neutral' Belgium that brought Britain into the war.) The idea of their 'Schlieffen Plan' was to drive into France on this wide front and then wheel round on Paris from the north, like a hammerhead, to deliver the crushing blow. It was to be so quick that the French would have no time to resist; the war with France would be over in six weeks. The German forces would then be free to combat the massive Russian forces to the east – it was anticipated that Russia would take at least 60 days to mobilize her armies.

The plan failed. The Russians managed to get a makeshift army in the field in 15 days. Though they were soon beaten back by German troops, and suffered a terrible defeat at Tannenberg, their efforts had drawn valuable troops away from the crucial

'hammerhead' in the west.

A second unforeseen factor was Britain's decision to join the war. Germany had not expected this, for in the build-up to hostilities Britain had seemed aloof, and they regarded the intervention as a betrayal.

However, for the first four weeks of the war, the Schlieffen Plan succeeded. By the end of August, the German armies had advanced far into France, and the French were retreating at breakneck speed. Then, on 5th September, the French armies commanded by Joffre decided to stand and fight. The two opposing forces were now barely 40 miles from Paris. The ensuing battle of the Marne was the most important engagement of the entire war, and was a decisive victory for the French, along with a small but well-trained force of British allies. The German advance was abruptly halted and they retreated to a line north of the River Aisne.

There, both sides dug themselves in. Two opposing lines of trenches, in some places barely 50 yards apart, stretched from the Alps to the sea. For the next four years, there was to be no further movement, except for the occasional 'push' as thousands of men were sacrificed to drive back the enemy at most a couple of miles on some short section of the Front.

Allied commanders were constantly launching 'pushes', the Germans less frequently. These futile attacks entailed 'going over the top' from trenches and stumbling across muddy ground, through shell-holes and ditches, before cutting rows of barbed wire – all the while under heavy shell and machine-gun fire. The numbers of men killed and wounded in the assaults were staggering. In the Allied offensive in Flanders, in the late summer of 1917, 400,000 men died in the mud around Passchendaele – many more were maimed for life. The offensive gained the Allies absolutely nothing.

## The impact of reality

On the 'home front', the attitude was, for much of the war, 'business as usual'. People tried stoically to work in the same way they had in peacetime. Artists, too, tried to carry on painting and writing – though composers often found they could not muster a full orchestra. Many artists, however, felt drained of inspiration; the monumental terror of the war somehow belittled their work. Gustave Holst was rejected from the army when he tried to volunteer, and felt useless as a result. Although he completed *The Planets* in 1917, the war was a period of intense depression and small output for him. Vaughan Williams enlisted in the Royal Army Medical Corps in 1914 and, although he did not go to France until 1916, the war so absorbed him that he wrote hardly any music at all. Even Elgar wrote only a little chamber music.

For some at the front, however, the realities of war served as a grim inspiration. The idealism soon fell from the eyes of those exposed to the unimaginable horrors of the trenches. By the middle of 1915, many hundreds of men were sending home poems or small volumes of verse from Flanders, Egypt and Turkey, cataloguing the terrible events they were witnessing. The sheer horror turned ordinary men into poets as they sought to express the depth of their reactions to the appalling suffering. And those who were already poets achieved a profundity in their writing they had never had before.

Much of the work is lost, stored away in attics,

*Perhaps because of the continual closeness of death, many entrenched soldiers experienced a heightened sensitivity to the sights they saw. And in the midst of destruction and horror they found elements of awesome beauty. 'Very' lights presented a nightly firework display above the trenches and white-hot bullets glowed like fireflies . . .*
*This strange beauty inspired Richard Nevinson to paint the stylized canvas,* **A Bursting Shell** *(centre). Nevinson started the war with a dispassionate fascination in the power of conflict and mechanized warfare. He was eventually made an official war artist. In the meantime, however, he lost his belief in the dignity of war.*

R. Nevinson 'Bursting Shell'. The Tate Gallery, London

buried in the French mud, or discarded long ago. Only the poems of the better-connected officers, such as Robert Graves, Isaac Rosenberg, Robert Nichols, Siegfried Sassoon and Wilfred Owen, survive. Realism and detailed description took the place of idealism, as in Rosenberg's *Dead Man's Dump:*

*The wheels lurched over sprawled dead*
*But pained them not, though their bones crunched,*
*Their shut mouths made no moan.*
*They lie there huddled, friend and foeman,*
*Man born of man, and born of woman,*
*And shells go crying over them*
*From night till night and now.*

Poetry like this was intended to prove to those back home that the glory of war was an illusion. It was intended to show what the men at the front were really suffering, and perhaps to act as a memorial to those who did not survive. It had its effect, but not as much as it might have – such poetry was not permitted, by government or media, to find wide publication – as witnessed by this passage from D. H. Lawrence's *Kangaroo:*

*It was in 1915 the old world ended . . . The integrity*
*of London collapsed and the genuine debasement*
*began, the unspeakable baseness of the press and*
*the public voice, the reign of that bloated ignominy,*
John Bull.

Not all artists found the experience of war so profoundly shocking or disillusioning. Futurist painters had, for a long time, found expressive power in the new machines of war like cars, guns and battleships and, in a way, gloried in the violence. Richard Nevinson, when rejected from the army as unfit, immediately joined the Belgian Red Cross and worked as an ambulance driver rather than be denied first-hand material for his paintings. But by the time he was employed as an official war artist, in 1917, even his belief in the 'beauty of strife' had been thoroughly shaken, and his paintings of the Western Front do not glorify mechanized war, but express human suffering instead.

### Despair and protest

By 1917, the war showed little sign of ever stopping. The casualties and suffering and waste of life seemed increasingly futile. A note of anguished despair crept into the work of many artists; their calls for a halt to the fighting became more and more strident.

In 1916, the Frenchman Henri Barbusse had written *Le Feu,* protesting at a war that had cost the lives of hundreds of thousands of Frenchman defending Verdun against constant bombardment. Barbusse's book was translated into English in 1917 and profoundly affected poets, such as Siegfried Sassoon and Wilfred Owen.

Sassoon's poems were simple, spontaneous expressions of anger at the war and the almost blasé callousness of the commanders who constantly sacrificed thousands of men in futile offensives.

*If I were fierce, and bald, and short of breath,*
*I'd live with scarlet Majors at the Base,*
*And speed glum heroes up the line to death.*
*You'd see me with my puffy petulant face,*
*Guzzling and gulping in the best hotel,*
*Reading the Roll of Honour. 'Poor young chap,'*
*I'd say – 'I used to know his father well;*
*Yes, we've lost heavily in this last scrap.'*
*And when the war is done and youth stone dead,*
*I'd toddle safely home and die – in bed.*

Sassoon's protests became so vocal and so specific that he was in danger of being court-martialled for treason. Fortunately, the army side-stepped the issue – perhaps because of Sassoon's distinguished war record – and invalided him out of the army to a hospital near Edinburgh. There he met Wilfred Owen.

Owen, like Sassoon, felt the need to protest. He wrote from the Front in 1917, 'The people of England needn't hope. They must agitate.' But it was not until he met Sassoon that he was confirmed in his resolve to speak out. Owen began to write a series of brilliant, searing indictments of the war and when his convalescence was over, he returned to the Front with almost missionary zeal. 'There I shall be better able to cry my outcry,' he wrote. In this verse from

BBC Hulton Picture Library

BBC Hulton Picture Library

Bayerisches Armeemuseum, Ingolstadt

*Insensibility* he echoes Sassoon's sentiments:

*Happy are men who yet before they are killed*
*Can let their veins run cold.*
*Whom no compassion fleers*
*Or makes their feet*
*Sore on the alleys cobbled with their brothers.*
*The front line withers.*
*But they are troops who fade, not flowers,*
*For poets' tearful fooling:*
*Men, gaps for filling:*
*Losses, who might have fought*
*Longer; but no one bothers.*

Tragically, Owen was killed less than three months later – and just one week before armistice. Today his poetry remains as a powerful epitaph to the horror, suffering and mindless waste of war.

### The end of the war

In the end it was not any 'big push' on land that defeated the Germans, but the stranglehold of the British Navy on the seas. The British blockade was so effective that, despite remarkable ingenuity in finding substitute materials and food, the Germans were simply starved into submission. In a desperate attempt to break the blockade, they resorted to submarine warfare. The sinking of the American civilian liner, *Lusitania* in 1915 outraged America; and continued unrestricted warfare against American shipping finally brought America into the war against Germany in 1917. This intervention tipped the balance decidedly in favour of the Allies, and Germany, already reduced by the terrible news from the Front and the privations at home, began to crumble. Many Germans were actually starving. By the end of 1918, in the face of internal collapse, Germany was obliged to sue for peace.

Fighting ceased on 11th November 1918 after more than four years of bloody conflict.

Disillusionment and horror had long since dis-placed the heady idealism and had been replaced in turn by anger. When the armistice was finally signed in December 1918, those artists who had pent up their feelings, loosed them in a torrent, and the post-war months were punctuated by the publication of the memoirs of men determined to reveal the truth about war, and so prevent it ever recurring. Robert Graves' *Goodbye to All That,* Blunden's *Undertones of War,* Montague's *Disenchantment* and Erich Maria Remarque's *All Quiet on the Western Front* are among the best known works of the post-war period.

Other artists – particularly painters and those involved in the performing arts – adopted a hedonistic outlook in response to the proven transience of youth and pleasure.

Perhaps their feelings are summed-up best by Wilfred Owen's allegorical retelling of the biblical story of Abraham and Isaac, *The Parable of the Old Men and the Young.* Those responsible for the War and its mismanagement are likened to Abraham; the young soldiers to the son Abraham was prepared to sacrifice. But Owen's poem reaches a dramatic and poignantly different conclusion from the Bible story:

*Then Abram bound the youth with belts and straps,*
*And builded parapets and trenches there,*
*And stretched forth the knife to slay his son.*
*When lo! an angel called him out of heaven,*
*Saying, Lay not thy hand upon the lad,*
*Neither do anything to him. Behold,*
*A ram, caught in a thicket by its horns;*
*Offer the ram of Pride instead of him.*
*But the old man would not so, but slew his son _*
*And half the seed of Europe, one by one.*

Nine of Wilfred Owen's poems formed the structure of Benjamin Britten's *War Requiem,* first performed in 1962. And its power to stir a generation a lifetime removed from the horror of the Great War, reveals the massive cultural scar left by that 'war to end all wars'.

*The skeleton of Chateau Woods, Ypres (left), laid bare by the attrition of massive daily bombardment. By the end of the War, artists, poets and writers were producing work as bleak and brutal as the battered landscape, in bitter protest at the cavalier and senseless squandering of life by commanders and politicians.*

# THE GREAT COMPOSERS

# *Sergei Prokofiev*
## *(1891–1953)*

# *Dmitri Shostakovich*
## *(1906–1975)*

*Sergei Prokofiev and Dmitri Shostakovich led Russian music into the modern era. The two composers suffered government criticism for their works, which Russian officials described as unharmonious and chaotic. Yet Prokofiev and Shostakovich rose above the criticism, composing some of the 20th century's most sophisticated and modern works. Prokofiev sought to provoke and even shock the listener with his dramatic works. Shostakovich, however, worked his way through the avant garde to settle in a concentrated, direct style. Although written during times of war and revolution, Prokofiev's Classical Symphony and Shostakovich's Symphony no. 9 in E Flat, both examined in the* Listener's Guide *with Prokofiev's Love of Three Oranges Suite, are light and charming orchestral works. The music of both composers was influenced by the changing political face of Russia;* In The Background *examines the fall of the last Tsar and the surge towards revolution.*

*Under the strict artistic limitations of post-revolutionary Russia worked two of its finest composers, Sergei Prokofiev and Dmitri Shostakovich. Prokofiev was born in Sontsovka in the Ukraine. He had a precocious talent; upon entering the St. Petersburg Conservatoire in 1904, he had already completed several works. His supreme self-confidence in his abilities, however, led to as many clashes as his compositions would in later years. After a successful period abroad, he settled in Moscow in 1936, composing prolifically but subject to the waves of government pressure; he died in 1953. Shostakovich was well aware of the artistic pressure imposed upon contemporaries like Prokofiev, for he lived in Russia for much of his life. His remarkable talents were shaped at the St. Petersburg Conservatoire, and he became an international success. But as his musical voice emerged, he found himself in and out of favour with the government. He died in 1975.*

## COMPOSER'S LIFE
# 'Twin giants'

**Prokofiev and Shostakovich rose above the
sometimes severe artistic limitations imposed on
them by the state to become the twin giants of
20th-century Soviet music.**

When the government of the Tsar finally fell in February 1917 and the long-awaited Russian Revolution exploded into life, Sergei Prokofiev was barely 26 years old and had recently graduated from the St Petersburg Conservatory ; Dmitri Shostakovich was just 11 and soon to enter the Conservatory. As the new Soviet state thrust its way forcefully into the world, so began the careers of its two foremost composers.

The Revolution had a cataclysmic effect on Russian life, but for artists one of the most important was the dramatically extended role of the state in the direction of art. In the early days of the Soviet Union, under Lenin's Commisar for the Arts, Anatoly Lunacharsky,

the state influence was positively liberating, for artists were no longer bound by the whims of the market place. Soviet artists responded to their new freedom with verve and originality, and in the 1920s Soviet art was amongst the most radical and innovative in the world.

But within the very freedom of early Soviet art lay the seeds of its eventual confinement. Radical art is inevitably anti-establishment, and it was not long before the new Soviet system itself was established enough to be attacked. At the same time the authorities sensed that all the experimentation was not contributing to the Revolution. Increasingly, after Joseph Stalin came to power, the Soviet

*Sergei Prokofiev (above left) lived abroad after the 1917 Revolution but returned to the Soviet Union in 1936. Initially he thought the cultural policies of the new state liberating but later found them highly restrictive. Dmitri Shostakovich (above) felt he had a moral duty to write for the state. Even so, his music did not escape criticism.*

government began to take the hard line advocated by those who favoured a *proletkult* – a proletarian culture rejecting all art that did not directly serve the revolutionary cause and the people.

The term 'Socialist Realism' was adopted in the early 1930s to describe the type of art the government wanted from Soviet artists. Artists were to show in a simple and direct – and essentially traditional – way, the achievement of the Soviet state and people. Throughout the lives of both Prokofiev and Shostakovich the guiding hand of the Central Committee of the Communist Party was an ever-present force, sometimes gently persuasive, sometimes ruthlessly dictatorial. Such was the political climate in which both composers lived and wrote their wonderful music.

## Sergei Prokofiev (1891–1953)

Always deeply intellectual but with a mischievous sense of humour, Sergei Prokofiev seemed to delight in shocking people with his music. In the pre-Revolutionary days he was very much the *enfant terrible* of Russian music and his compositions were shocking to ears accustomed to the more lilting and romantic music of many early 20th century composers.

Prokofiev was born on 23 April 1891 at Sontsovka in the Ukraine on the estate managed by his father. His mother, Maria, loved playing the piano and naturally Sergei was introduced to the piano at a very early age. She was a good teacher and Sergei had a precocious talent – by the age of six he could play the piano fluently. By the age of seven he had composed his first orchestrated piano piece, a march in C for four hands, and at nine he had written his first opera, *The Giant*.

Sontsovka was an attractive place to grow up and Prokofiev seems to have had a happy childhood there. He revelled not only in the pleasures of the countryside but in devising and staging plays with his friends from the village.

Rapid though his musical progress was, however, his mother realized that he needed extra tuition. After hearing Sergei play, the brilliant eccentric of Russian music, Sergei Taneyev recommended that she engage the young composer Reinhold Glière to coach Sergei at Sontsovka. From the summer of 1902 at regular intervals over the next two years Glière came to Sontsovka to teach him the basics of composition. Sergei's knowledge of what was current in music came from both Glière and his annual visits to Moscow with his mother. He made good progress with composition and in 1904 when he applied to the St Petersburg Conservatory at the age of 13, he took with him a portfolio of four operas, two sonatas, a symphony and many other pieces.

His ten years at the Conservatory were stormy, and at one time or other Prokofiev seemed to clash with virtually everyone. This was partly because he already felt himself to be a composer who needed little but polishing up and partly because of the innate conservatism of his teachers.

In 1910 his father died and although he continued to live with his mother in St Petersburg, receiving financial support from her, it was now obvious that he would have to make his own way. Fortunately, 1911 marked the beginning of his recognition beyond the immediate circle of family, friends and the Conservatory. In 1911 and 1913 his First and Second Piano Concertos were premièred, each causing a stir.

Novosti

H. Roger-Viollet

*Prokofiev (left) had a very happy childhood on the estate at Sontsovka which his father managed. Apart from his musical pursuits – by the time he was 11 he had written two operas and many piano pieces – he excelled at chess.*

*Prokofiev's first visit to Paris (below) in 1920 was a great success. From then until 1936, except for a few absences, his life and work centred on Paris.*

*Prokofiev (above) met his wife Lina Llubera (left) on his first visit to America in 1920. They were married in 1923 and had two sons, Svyatoslav and Oleg.*

*Vsevolod Meyerbold (below right), an avant-garde theatre director, was a friend of both Prokofiev and Sbostakovich. His creativity, like that of many others, posed a threat to Stalin who arrested him in 1939.*

His music appeared in print for the first time and in 1914 he graduated, winning the Rubinstein Prize for a performance of his *First Piano Concerto.*

### The composer abroad

As a reward for graduating his mother paid for him to have a holiday in London. While there in 1914 he saw and was intoxicated by Diaghilev's Ballets Russes at their spectacular best. A chance meeting with the great impresario himself led to a commission for a ballet on a Russian subject. However, he could not get a clear picture of what was needed and his first attempt was rejected by Diaghilev; his second, called *The Tale of the Buffoon,* with a plot agreed on by the composer and Diaghilev was more successful and received its first performance after World War I.

During the war Prokofiev returned to the Conservatory as a student to avoid being conscripted. During this period he produced many works including *The Scythian Suite* and, in the year of the Revolution, 1917, the famous *Classical Symphony.*

His reaction to the Revolution was favourable but restrained. But soon he began to feel that the new Soviet state would have more important things to think about than new music and in May 1918 he obtained permission from the Commissar for the Arts, Lunacharsky, to go abroad for a while. It was not an easy time to travel, for Europe was still at war and he was stuck in Tokyo for months, en route to America.

Initially he was well-received in America. As a result of his first recital the company which made Steinway-Duo-art player pianos asked him to record for them. He was also commissioned to write some

piano works by a New York publishing house. However, he concentrated on the completion and production of his opera *The Love of Three Oranges* so exclusively that many of his contacts dried up. In any case he soon became disillusioned with the sheer commercialism of the American musical scene. But there was some consolation – while in New York he fell in love with an attractive singer of mixed Spanish and Russian origin, Lina Llubera. She later became his wife, but in 1920 Prokofiev headed for Paris, where in 1921 his ballet, *The Tale of the Buffoon* delighted Paris audiences. After a trip to America in October 1921 for rehearsals and the première in Chicago of *The Love of Three Oranges,* Prokofiev returned to Europe and settled in 1922 in the small Bavarian village of Ettal.

After his marriage to Lina in 1923 the family moved to Paris. Early in 1923 he had been invited to return to Russia for a concert series but with his family ties in Europe – his mother, now elderly and ill, was living with him – he felt unable to accept.

In official music circles in Russia he was held in some suspicion, but was strongly defended by his friends. At this stage in his life his future in Europe looked extremely promising – he was at the height of his fame both as a composer and a pianist. By 1925 when he returned again to America his European reputation went ahead of him and his music was treated much more seriously than on his first visit. To complete the happy picture Lina had borne him two sons, Svyatoslav in 1924 and Oleg in 1928.

In 1929, at the invitation of his friend Meyerhold, he returned to Russia in the face of considerable

90

hostility from the Russian Association of Proletarian Musicians (RAPM). He was at the time recovering from an injury to his hands so did not perform. He was, however, able to renew friendships and to gain a closer knowledge of the state of music in Russia. Over the next few years he toured in Europe and America and visited Russia a number of times. Although RAPM regarded him as a corrupted, Westernized composer, Prokofiev began to think more and more about living in Russia permanently. He continued to live in Paris officially, but from 1933 he had a flat in Moscow and in 1936 took up permanent residence there.

### Return to the Soviet Union

The reasons for his decision to return are not altogether clear. It seems though, that his increasing disillusionment with Western music played a large part. Back in the Soviet Union his music became much softer – some said it lost its fire – as he strove to make his music more accessible to people. Compositions such as *Romeo and Juliet* and the music for the film *Alexander Nevsky* contain passages of warm lyricism rarely heard in his earlier work. However, he did not stop writing difficult music altogether and claimed in 1935 that he wrote two kinds of music – one for the masses and one for posterity.

*Prokofiev began working on his opera* War and Peace *(a sketch for an Italian production, below) in 1941 at Nalchik, one of the places to which many Soviet composers were evacuated during World War 2. His original plan was that the opera should be on an intimate personal scale, showing the development of the main characters of Tolstoy's novel. But by the time he had revised it on the advice of the Committee of the Arts in Moscow it had become an epic work. He revised and changed it many times after that and it was only after his death that a more or less complete version was performed in Russia.*

8814. P. Z. -ST-PETERSBOURG.

Design by Bozzetto di Scitian. Photo Mauro Pucciarelli-Rome

ВОЙНА и МИР.

Despite the prolific rate at which he wrote, these years were not entirely happy ones for him. He had seen his friends and colleagues abused by Stalin's agents; some like Shostakovich, publicly pilloried, others, like Tukhachevsky and Meyerhold, executed. Prokofiev survived by working harder than ever. 'Today one must work. Work is the only thing, the only salvation' he would repeat to himself. The strain of so much work and tension proved too much for his health and in 1941 he suffered a heart attack.

During World War 2 he worked quietly and steadily at Nalchik, where many Soviet composers had been sent for safety. He was accompanied there by Mira Mendelson. Secrecy surrounds the split with his wife, Lina, and his subsequent relationship with Mira. The Soviet biographer Victor Seroff suggested that Lina, as a flamboyant foreigner with friends in Germany, was a dangerous connection. Prokofiev's

relationship with Mira, who had friends in the Communist party, was thought to be politically convenient. Possibly it was an essential step to save him and his children and, perhaps, Lina herself, from the Soviet Authorities. Lina, however, did not escape and was arrested as a spy and sent to a labour camp.

Whatever the truth, the relationship with Mira was not enough to save Prokofiev from the second wave of purges in 1947. Along with Shostakovich and Khachaturian and many others he was hauled before the Central Committee of the party, headed by Zhdanov, and made to write a detailed confession of his failure to live up to the ideals of Socialist Realism.

By now he was in poor health and little able to put up much of a fight. His musical output dropped rapidly and he spent much of his time reworking previous compositions, such as *War and Peace.*

*The Fotomas Index*

*Dmitri Shostakovich was born in 1906 in St Petersburg, later renamed Petrograd, then Leningrad (left), where he lived for much of his life. He entered the Conservatory there in 1919 and wrote his First Symphony as a graduation piece in 1924. Here he spent the first few months after the German invasion in 1941 before being evacuated from the besieged city. During those months he wrote the first three movements of the Seventh Symphony, which he later dedicated to Leningrad. The 'Leningrad' Symphony as it came to be known was smuggled out of Russia and broadcast on American radio in July 1942. It became a symbol to all the Allies of resistance to the evils of Nazism.*

leading representative of Soviet art. The relationship between state and composer, however, was far from easy and was to cause him considerable anguish.

He was born, on 25 September 1906, in St Petersburg just a year after the violent but unsuccessful uprising of 1905. His father, also called Dmitri, was a small, rather jolly engineer of Polish origin. Dmitri senior may not have been a revolutionary himself, but he had been born in an exiles' camp where his father had been sent for his part in the assassination of Tsar Alexander II in 1881. Naturally, the young composer grew up fully aware of the political issues of the day and was committed to the idea of revolution. It is significant that his first composition, written in 1916 at the age of ten, was called *Soldier*. A year later, during the Revolution, he wrote the *Funeral March in Memory of the Victims of the Revolution*.

Remarkably, when he composed these pieces, he had been learning to play the piano for little more than a year. Before the age of nine, although he used to listen to amateur music-makers in the neighbouring flat, he had no desire to learn to play himself. However, his mother Sophia, a passionate music lover and a highly accomplished pianist, overcame his resistance and persuaded him to start piano lessons. Once he began to play, he soon learned to love it and proved to have a remarkable talent.

In 1919, at the age of 13, he enrolled at the Conservatory. Although civil war was raging throughout the country, teaching at the Conservatory went on much as normal, for Lenin valued the arts highly and spared as much of the meagre resources of the new state as possible for that purpose. However, in his third year, shortly before he began to study full time, the Shostakovich family suffered a tremendous blow. In February 1922, Dmitri senior died suddenly.

The composer's mother Sophia managed to get a job typing for the Chamber of Weights and Measures and his elder sister gave music lessons. But it was still barely enough to survive on. Then, a year later, Shostakovich was found to have tuberculosis. An operation seemed to alleviate the worst symptoms, but he was often in poor health subsequently. A further blow followed in 1924 when Sophia was dismissed from her job and was unable to find another. Dmitri decided to go to work himself. He took a job playing the piano three nights a week at the local 'Bright Reel' cinema to accompany the films and loathed every minute of it.

During that unhappy winter he began working on his brilliant *First Symphony*. The symphony was completed 18 months later – when he was just 19 – and took the musical world by storm. He submitted it to the Conservatory as his graduation piece and the examiners were so overwhelmed by its power that they arranged a full performance. The première, in Leningrad on May 12 1926, was just the first of many triumphant Shostakovich premières to come.

The Soviet authorities immediately took the young composer to their hearts as the torch-bearer of Soviet art. As the Moscow *Evening Radio* explained, '. . . The absence of the great leaders of our music who have emigrated abroad (Stravinsky, Rachmaninov and Prokofiev) doesn't frighten us. They have successors.' It was a responsibility that was to bear heavily on the composer in years to come.

Premières of the symphony were arranged in Moscow and then cities all across Europe. Soon Shostakovich was an international star. Financially secure at last, he started to write prolifically, writing

There was one notable suite, *On Guard for Peace*, his first major composition on a topical Soviet issue – it was awarded the Stalin Prize in 1950. During his last years Prokofiev was unable to leave his Moscow apartment for more than an hour or two without medical attention. He died on 6 March 1953 just three hours before Stalin. His death passed almost unnoticed by a nation plunged into official mourning for the dictator who had controlled it for so long.

## Dmitri Shostakovich (1906–1975)

Living under the Soviet system for all but his first 11 years, Shostakovich was a truly Soviet composer, always deeply committed to the socialist ideal, committed too to the concept of Social Realism, and the state responded by promoting him abroad as the

*Joseph Stalin (below, lying in state) died on 6 March 1953 just three hours after Prokofiev. Both Shostakovich and Prokofiev had suffered along with many other artists in Stalin's purges. These were designed to ensure that the arts reflected the political aims of the state. After Stalin's death Shostakovich found that conditions eased and he began to write more prolifically.*

*Popperfoto*

Novosti

When Hitler invaded Russia in 1941, Shostakovich was in Leningrad where he was as passionate in defence of his country against the Nazis as anyone. He was refused permission to join the army, but insisted on staying on in Leningrad when the long German siege began. As the people of Leningrad's heroic resistance continued, under increasingly desperate conditions, Shostakovich began writing a symphony as a testimony to their courage.

The success of the 'Leningrad' Symphony (Shostakovich's Seventh) was remarkable, for even as it was being composed it became the very symbol of Russian resistance. At the première in Moscow, the audience refused to interrupt their ovation to the composer even for an air-raid. For the première in Leningrad, a heroic effort by the soldiers defending the city managed to silence the German guns for the duration of the performance.

another two symphonies, two ballets, *The Golden Age* and *Bolt,* and an opera *The Nose,* as well as many other pieces during the next five years. It was a relatively happy period for the young composer, although the strain of constant public appearances drove him to chain smoking. In 1932, he married his first wife Nina Varzar and in 1936 a daughter, Galya, was born; a son, Maxim, later to be a conductor and one of his father's best interpreters, was born in 1938.

But while he was working on his next major work, an opera which was to be a Russian version of Shakespeare's Lady Macbeth, there were the first ominous rumblings in the Party against modernism and similar bourgeois attitudes. The opera was completed and was performed both at home and abroad in the years 1934 to 1936 with tremendous success, firmly establishing Shostakovich's reputation. Then early in 1936, an article appeared in the newspaper *Pravda,* under the heading 'Chaos instead of Music' condemning Shostakovich's opera as grinding 'progressive' confusion. Such a denunciation in the official Party organ meant big trouble.

The problem seemed to be that *Lady Macbeth of the Msensk District* was a tragedy, even though a tragedy of life under the Tsar, and was not, as Socialist Realist music should be, uplifting. Soon Shostakovich found other works of his, such as his new ballet *The Limpid Stream,* condemned as well. At a time when Stalin's purges were beginning to bite, this was frightening and he immediately withdrew his tragic *Fourth Symphony,* then about to go into rehearsal. Later in the year, he was hauled before the Union of Soviet composers to answer to his 'crimes'. After much heated debate, the union agreed to help him back on to the straight and narrow.

Shostakovich was forced to rethink his approach – though he was probably rethinking it anyway – and with his next symphony, the Fifth, he redeemed himself in the eyes of the authorities. It was heroic, used simpler harmonies, had a happy ending and was a tremendous success. It came to be known by a sub-title 'A Soviet artist's reply to just criticism,' and gave the impression, at least, that he had returned to the fold. Yet as he wrote this extrovert public music, so he was starting to work on a remarkable series of introverted, emotional string quartets.

*Shostakovich and his first wife Nina, photographed with their good friend Ivan Sollertinsky (above) in the year of their marriage, 1932. They had two children: a daughter, Galya, and a son, Maxim (top right). Maxim became a conductor and is thought to be one of the best interpreters of his father's work.*

*Shostakovich's opera Katerina Izmaylova (the wedding scene from the 1963 Covent Garden production is shown right) was first performed in Leningrad in 1934 where it was successfully received. However by 1936 he was the subject of attack in a newspaper article entitled 'Chaos instead of music'. Pravda, the newspaper in which the article appeared was the official Soviet Party organ and this signalled the beginning of his problems with the authorities.*

*The poster (far right) dated 1920 celebrates the victory of the people over the Imperial system and reflects the beginnings of a new social order – a new order that was to have artistic repercussions for both Prokofiev and Shostakovich.*

But his triumph was to be short-lived, perhaps because he celebrated the end of the war with a light, joyful little symphony (his Ninth), rather than the big, heroic work that was expected of him. In 1948, he again became a target for official criticism, along with many other Soviet composers. This time the treatment was more severe and Shostakovich was forced to write a long confession of his guilt to charges of formalism – the crime of putting form higher than content or message. He was obliged to condemn all the music he had written previously.

That this was immensely difficult is evident in the fact that during the next five years he wrote little of significance. Instead he became a spokesman for peace, attending many conferences and delegations all round the world. For his contributions here he was awarded the Nobel Peace Prize.

Although all had been published before, bringing them together in a symphony seemed to highlight their controversial nature – they condemned anti-Semitism, praised non-conformism and criticized the police state.

Throughout his final years, Shostakovich remained continuously creative, but his music became increasingly divided into 'public' music and introspective 'private' music. Even in the symphonies, a chill note creeps in and these years seem to be marked by a profound isolation – though he was now happily married to his third wife, Irena Suprinskaya, and was the subject of numerous television documentaries, articles in the press and a figure very much in the public eye.

Since 1966 he had been in poor health, suffering first from a heart ailment and later from arthritis, and on 9 August 1975 he died after a heart attack.

Then in 1953, the year of Stalin's death, he 'redeemed' himself yet again with the emotional *Tenth Symphony*. With Stalin's death, conditions eased and Shostakovich began writing prolifically once more, although he became notably more introverted. Events in his personal life probably contributed to his introversion. In 1954 his wife Nina died and in 1955 his mother died. His second marriage in 1956 was unhappy and short-lived. However his *Eleventh Symphony*, written to celebrate the 40th anniversary of the revolution in October 1957, was another success and Shostakovich, after ten lean years, was a celebrity once more.

In 1962 he ran foul of the authorities again by the result of a collaboration with the young poet Yevgeni Yevtushenko. He created a symphony with a chorus of five of Yevtushenko's poems set to music.

# Orchestral works

**_Despite being written against the grim backdrop of war, Prokofiev's 'Classical' and Shostakovich's Ninth symphonies are the lightest and most charming of their large orchestral works._**

## The Classical Symphony

When Sergei Prokofiev sat down to write the Classical Symphony in the summer of 1916, he was on the threshold of a career as an internationally renowned composer. Indeed, in many ways, it was his bid for stardom. That it succeeded so well is a tribute to his precocious talent, and perhaps also to western society's taste for sophisticated music. Prokofiev's symphony is a perfect blend of the frivolous elegance of classical music and his own distinctive, quintessentially 20th-century music.

Prokofiev was 25 years old when he wrote the symphony and was already known abroad through the success of his _Scythian Suite_. But it was the Classical Symphony that permanently established his reputation and paved the way for his subsequent emigration from Russia. Indeed, it was just a few days after the first performance of the symphony in Petrograd in May 1918 that Prokofiev asked permission from the Soviet Commissar for the Arts, Anatoly Lunacharsky, to leave the country.

At the time Prokofiev wrote the Classical Symphony, World War I was bringing terrible suffering to millions of people all over the world and to Russians in particular. And as Prokofiev was finishing the piece in 1917, Russia was going through the violent and turbulent revolution that brought the Soviet state into being. Yet while these cataclysmic events were taking place, Prokofiev went on working quietly and productively in a quiet village on the outskirts of Petrograd. And the Classical Symphony bears no hint of either the War or the Revolution – a striking contrast with Shostakovich, living and working in the same city in World War II and writing a symphony (his Seventh), that summed up the heroic resistance of the people of Leningrad to the German assault. Prokofiev preferred to distance himself from world events.

In his country retreat, where he spent the time reading the philosophies of Immanuel Kant and composing, Prokofiev set out to create an elegant symphony in the style of Haydn:

_. . . It seemed to me that had Haydn lived in our day he would have retained his own style while accepting something of the new at the same time. That was the kind of symphony I wanted to write: a symphony in the classical style. And when I saw that my idea was beginning to_

work, I called it the 'Classical Symphony' _. . . in the first place because it was simpler, and secondly, for the fun of it, to 'tease the geese', and in the secret hope that I would prove to be right if the symphony really did turn out to be a piece of classical music._

In the end, it was both more and less than Prokofiev intended. On the one hand, it seems to lack the emotional warmth of a Haydn symphony. On the other, it is an affectionate, witty and sardonic pastiche of the classical tradition. More than that, it has a very 20th-century dynamism and approach to harmony. Although tame by Stravinsky's standards, the harmonies were still strikingly dissonant and exciting to the musical public of the time. This, combined with the powerful rhythms, gives the classical froth a thrilling edge.

In composing this symphony, Prokofiev made a deliberate change in his working methods:

_I deliberately did not take my piano with me ( to the retreat), for I wished to try composing without it. Until this time, I had always composed at the piano, but I noticed that the thematic material composed away from the piano was often better. At first it seemed strange when transferred to the piano, but after one has played it a few times, everything falls into place. I had been toying with the idea of writing a whole symphony without the piano – I believed that the orchestra would sound more natural. That is how the project . . . came into being._

Prokofiev claims to have written the symphony in his head while walking in the country. As Prokofiev was working on the symphony, the crisis in Petrograd was coming to a head. Soon after the Symphony was finished, Lenin seized power in Moscow and the country was plunged into civil war. There was no prospect of an immediate première, and Prokofiev went to his mother's house in the country at Kislovodsk in the Caucasus Mountains. When Kislovodsk fell into Red Russian hands in March 1918, Prokofiev immediately headed back north, first to Moscow and then to Petrograd where he was able to give the Classical Symphony its first performance in May. It was soon in great demand all over the world, and has become one of the most popular of all 20th century symphonies.

Cesare Detti 'The Departure'. Fine Art Photographic

## Programme notes

The Classical Symphony is written for the size of orchestra Haydn or Mozart would have used: two flutes, two oboes, two clarinets, two bassoons, two horns, two trumpets, tympani and strings. The structure of the piece too is strictly classical, with a first movement in 'sonata form' and the traditional four movement progression – from dramatic first movement, through lyrical second movement, a dance-like third movement, to a stirring finale.

Yet despite these similarities, the harmonies are much freer and more modern than those of the Viennese masters and the instrumentation while transparently clear, is far more detailed.

### 1st movement: allegro

The first movement is in the classic sonata form used by Haydn and Mozart, with the three part division into exposition, development, and recapitulation so well

*Like so much of Prokofiev's early work, the Classical Symphony is filled with a frivolity and sly humour lacking in much early 20th century music. It captures perfectly the frothy, elegant, rather fanciful gaiety that characterizes our image of Vienna in the classical era (left).*

*The cultured lightness of the Classical Symphony seems to fit ill with the sombre Russian landscape in which Prokofiev was brought up. And yet even in this very urban music, there are faint echoes of the wild, ancient rhythms and melodies of the Russian countryside (below).*

defined that it is a joy to follow the structure. The first theme or 'subject' is highly memorable.

Example 1

It is rattled off on the strings, with wispy phrases on the woodwind beautifully dove-tailed in, and a solo flute prominent. The second subject on the violin is directed to be played *con eleganza, sul punto del' arco* (elegantly, with the point of the bow).

Example 2

Pietro Longhi 'Dancing Lesson: The Gavotte' Mauro Pucciarelli-Rome

The tic-toc accompaniment on the bassoon recalls Haydn's Clock Symphony.

After a clearly marked pause, the development starts, and the second theme is treated in syncopation by the full orchestra. With an unusually powerful climbing assertion, for such a small-scale work, on trumpets and horns, the recapitulation is reached.

### 2nd movement: larghetto

Over a quiet accompaniment on the strings, the first violins play *molto dolce* (very sweetly) a long drawn out melody with a beautiful flickering semi-quaver passage between its two sections. When the flute plays its version of this melody the flickering effect becomes quite exquisite.

The second section is marked *tranquillo* (quietly), and strings pluck quietly away. As it builds gradually to a climax, a new theme enters on the bassoon, before a return to the first graceful melody. Towards the very end of the movement, Prokofiev's striking modernity of orchestration within

*The delicate gavotte of the Third Movement of the Classical Symphony paints a pretty picture of the refined, courtly dances of Viennese society in the time of Haydn (above).*

the rigid classical framework comes to the fore, as the oboe provides an incredibly elaborate accompaniment to the flute.

### 3rd movement: gavotta non troppo allegro

The dance theme with its deliberate four beat rhythm is played by the violins to a woodwind accompaniment and the second section is repeated. The middle section has a lovely theme on oboe before the flute introduces an elegant 'gavotte' – a courtly dance popular in the 18th century. There follows a delicate restrained ending, with pizzicato closing notes on the strings displaying the height of good manners.

### 4th movement: Finale, molto vivace

The finale is full of drive and momentum; it is a miracle of invention and dynamic

## Understanding music: Neo-classicism

It must have seemed to many that, after *The Rite of Spring,* musical revolution could be carried no further. But often, forward-looking movements in the arts are followed by movements backward. So it was that around 1920, composers began to look back to the forms and styles of earlier music. The movement, known as 'Neo-classicism', fused new developments with old models. For, as Prokofiev's 'Classical' symphony shows, that was the essence of neo-classicism – a re-interpretation of the distant past in the light of the present.

This sort of re-interpretation could be very direct, as when Stravinsky created in 1920, his ballet, *Pulcinella.* This was a pastiche of music by, or supposedly by, the 18th-century Neapolitan, Pergolesi, which Diaghilev had introduced to Stravinsky. The ballet, which was choreographed by Massine and had sets designed by Picasso, featured the *commedia dell'arte* characters, Harlequin, Columbine, etc. The work is a deliberate distortion of the original, using 'inappropriate' instruments, adding rhythmic zest and harmonic spice. So, though the outlines are classical, the music belongs very much to the 20th century. Although there had been Neo-classical works before – notably Prokofiev's symphony – it was Stravinsky's Neo-classicism that most impressed his contemporaries and proved a very significant feature of musical development by providing a gateway to the past.

Once through that gateway, Stravinsky began to create new works owing something to past styles; and since Bach's music seemed to embody the strictest style, it was to Bach that Stravinsky first turned. His need was for order, and he found that order in Bach's even phrasing, counterpoint and exactly-balanced forms. The influence was especially prominent in works of the 1920s and after, such as the ballet, *Apollon Musagètes* (later to be known merely as *Apollo*) in which he paid homage to the Age of Enlightenment and Reason, and the *Concerto in E flat* for chamber orchestra (1938), popularly known as 'Dumbarton Oaks'. Such pieces are immediately recognizable as Stravinsky's, even though they are very different from the music he was writing before World War I, for here, the references to the 18th century are absolutely clear.

Apart from Stravinsky and Prokofiev, other composers to take the 'Back to Bach' path included the German, Paul Hindemith (1895–1903) and Bartók. Hindemith wrote several concertos and chamber music in the Neo-classical style where the harmonic weight is pushed forward by energetic Bachian rhythm. In his *Kammermusiken nos. 2–7* (1924–7), he highlights solo instruments as in the 'Brandenburg' concertos, while movements in the 'Fourth string quartet' are marked fugue, chorale prelude, march and passacaglia. Similarly, Bartók showed his admiration for the clarity of Baroque counterpoint in works such as his *Second Piano Concerto.*

Neo-classicism was a general trend in all the arts between the World Wars. It can be found in the painting of Picasso as much as in the music of Stravinsky. It can even be found in the works of Schoenberg, who was influenced by Neo-classicism though he deplored it in Stravinsky. In works such as the *Piano Suite, op. 25* (1921–3) and the *Wind Quintet, op. 26* (1924), he wrote with much greater contrapuntal and structural clarity than earlier works, and he acknowledged the influence by including, as Bach had done, the musical letters B-A-C-H in his score. He also made adaptations of 18th-century compositions in a style not very dissimilar to *Pulcinella.*

Yet another aspect of Schoenberg's Neo-classicism was his invention of 12-note serialism, which gave him the means to return to symphonic development in the line of the great Austrian tradition from Haydn to Brahms. His pupil Webern used serialism to different ends, but his music too shows the typical Neo-classical virtues of economy, evident counterpoint and formal simplicity.

While Hindemith, Bartók, Schoenberg and Webern were all concerned principally with Bach, Stravinsky's Neo-classicism became more comprehensive. As he had said of *Pulcinella,* stealing from the past was an expression of love, and as time went on, he came to love the classics even more. In his work we see the influence of Weber, whose brilliant piano style became a feature of his *Capriccio* for piano and orchestra (1929); Tchaikovsky, whose symphonies and ballets are often alluded to; and even medieval music, which has some bearing on the austere *Mass* for voices and wind instruments (1948). The climax of all this was the opera, *The Rake's Progress* (1951), in which Stravinsky very consciously worked within the framework of Mozart's comedies.

After this, Neo-classicism came to an end. Stravinsky found the more recent past of Schoenberg and Webern of greater interest; while the younger composers were no longer interested in abiding by the older order. Music had entered a further experimental phase.

By then, though, the musical world was so different that the term, 'Neo-classicism' could no longer be applied. It belongs, first and last, to those works of the 1920s, 30s and 40s in which the orderliness of the past was paraded as much as the dissension and confusion of the present.

energy. The opening theme bowls along with a sudden swirl on the clarinets above the strings. The second theme is reached with a very daring piece of writing; the woodwind plays the same note over and over again before launching into the melody. This section is repeated, giving another chance to enjoy its brilliance.

There follows a traditional classical 'development' of these themes as flute and woodwind subtly change and re-arrange them. This leads naturally into the 'recapitulation' section where the music returns to the original key and woodwind solos chase the strings in a joking fashion, marked *scherzando* (jokily) in the score. Throughout the movement Prokofiev uses bursts on the drum to keep things spinning along.

### The 'Love of Three Oranges' Suite

Prokofiev's orchestral suite Opus 33a was based on his ill-fated opera *The Love of Three Oranges.* He had started writing the opera en route to America in 1918, but illness prevented him from completing it until October 1919. The Chicago Opera were keen to perform it, but after three months of rehearsal, their director Camapanini died suddenly. It was not until late 1921, under the directorship of Mary Garden, that the opera finally reached the stage. It was hailed as a great success and was transferred to New York in February. But although the public loved it, New York critics gave it a terrible panning—some say simply because it was a Chicago company. After an all too brief run, the opera *Love of*

*Rabinovich's costume designs (right and below) for the opera 'The Love of Three Oranges', on which the orchestral suite was based, capture the strutting absurdity of 'Les Ridicules' (The ridiculous people).*

*Three Oranges* was taken off and it has been staged only rarely since then.

Despite the failure of the opera, Prokofiev was reluctant to abandon the material altogether and, in 1924, he completed both a piano score and an orchestral suite using the main themes from the opera, in order to give it a wider hearing. The Suite has since proved to be immensely popular and it is in this form that most people know the *Love of Three Oranges.*

### Programme notes

The central character of the opera is a sad Prince. The story tells how the Prince laughs at the Fairy Morgana, who punishes

him by putting a curse on him; he must go in search of three oranges with which he will fall in love.

The prince and his valet, Truffaldino, eventually locate the three oranges in the desert. While the Prince sleeps, the valet, overcome by thirst, opens one of the oranges. A beautiful Princess steps out, then faints, and dies of thirst. A second orange is opened, and a second Princess emerges to expire in the same way. Truffaldino panics, and takes flight. Then the prince wakes, opens the orange, and out comes the Princess Ninette. Just as she is about to die of thirst too, the 'Ridicules' bring a bucket of water, and the prince and princess declare their love for each other in a beautiful duet. After defeating the forces of evil, they marry, and live happily ever after.

The Suite is actually divided into six sections, each based on a theme from the opera. It opens with the absurd, strutting theme that characterizes *Les Ridicules* (the ridiculous people) before moving into the theme from the scene where the magician Tchello and the Fairy Morgana play cards in Hell. Here the music vividly conjures the swirling fires of Hell while rhythmic passages suggest the shuffling and dealing of the cards. The third section is a parody of heroic symphonic marches, notably the finale of Tchaikovsky's Sixth Symphony. A *scherzo* (joke) section then leads into a lyrical passage, rare in Prokofiev, beautifully creating an image of the courtship of the Prince and Princess, with woodwind and strings wooing each other tenderly. The Suite finishes with the couple's hectic flight from danger.

## Shostakovich: Symphony No. 9 in E Flat

Describing his Ninth Symphony, Shostakovich called it a merry little piece. 'Musicians will love to play it, and critics will delight in blasting it.' How right he was – although he had himself to blame for the disappointment and perplexity it caused. He had given rise to expectations that the Ninth Symphony was to be a celebration of victory, the culmination of a trio of symphonies programmed on the progress of World War 2. In his Seventh, the 'Leningrad' symphony, Shostakovich had dealt with the Nazi invasion of Russia, and in his Eighth, the suffering of war and the turning of the tide after Stalingrad. Both of these were mountainous symphonies using huge orchestras, and each lasting over an hour. And now, there was this 'molehill', lasting less than half an hour, and calling for a small orchestra of classical limits on the scale of, and in the style of, Prokofiev's Classical Symphony. 'We were prepared to listen to a new monumental fiasco . . . but we heard something quite different, something that at first astounded us by its unexpectedness,' commented a fellow musician.

It was composed in only six weeks at the

Soviet Composers' Rest Home near Ivanovo, 150 miles north east of Moscow, and immediately, on its first performance, brought Shostakovich into conflict with the musical establishment, and with Stalin himself. In his memoirs, Shostakovich related how the seething dissatisfaction with him grew to a climax. The Eighth symphony had already been criticized for being counter-revolutionary and anti-Soviet, for he had written an optimistic symphony at the beginning of the war when the Germans were winning, and a tragic one now they were losing, proving that he was on the side of the Fascists. Now everyone was expecting him to come out with a majestic Ninth symphony, an ode to Stalin, the great and successful leader, who with victory going to his head, was 'like a frog puffing himself up to the size of an ox.'

*Everyone praised Stalin, and now I was supposed to join in this unholy affair . . . and they demanded that Shostakovich use quadruple winds, choir, and soloists to hail the leader. All the more because Stalin found the number auspicious — the Ninth Symphony . . . I confess that I gave hope to the leader and teacher's dreams. I*

**The powerful stranglehold of the Russian leader Josef Stalin over Soviet cultural life, and in particular his efforts to stamp out 'corrupt' western ideas (characterized in this French cartoon from 1936, below), played a dominant role in Shostakovich's music for over 20 years. Yet Shostakovich's Ninth Symphony,** *instead of the heroic tribute Stalin expected, was a joyful celebration of the end of the War — its mood not of a triumphal victory march, but one of relief as the horrific merry-go-round of war (left) finally stopped.*

*announced that I was writing an apotheosis. I was trying to get them off my back, but it turned against me. When my ninth was performed Stalin was incensed.*

Now that the storm has settled, it is easier in retrospect to see what sort of victory Shostakovich was celebrating. The skittish, carefree nature of the work expresses a sense of irresponsible abandon rather than an official victory celebration. It conveys the spirit of soldiers being demobilized, knowing that not only will they not have to fight tomorrow, they won't even have to go on parade, or wear uniform. It is in fact a real victory symphony — a victory over militarism.

## Programme notes

### 1st movement: allegro

The movement starts off at breakneck speed with a terseness and compression reminiscent of a Haydn quartet — indeed it seems more like chamber music than a symphony, and as Sir Neville Cardus said, it is 'probably the least symphonic music ever written'.

The principal theme is hardly a melody.

Example 3

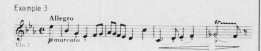

It might well have been a secondary theme in a classical symphony, skipping down to end with a pronounced trill. It is promptly stood on its head, tossed between flute and violin, then continued by a sarcastic oboe.

Then, with a blare of trombones giving a mock military band accompaniment, an irreverent contrasting theme is whistled

ASSOCIÉS

POUR QU'ELLE SOIT LIBRE, FORTE, HEUREUSE

Like children
dressing up as
soldiers (right),
Shostakovich's
Ninth Symphony is
a playful mockery
of militarism.
Although the
composer was
castigated by the
Soviet authorities
at the time for not
creating the
stirring music they
felt the Soviet
victory over the
Germans
deserved, it seems
in retrospect that
Shostakovich's
music was actually
more in tune with
the mood of the
Soviet people,
overjoyed at the
fact that the
fighting was finally
over.

Sir William McTaggart 'The Press Gang' Fine Art Photographic

by a piccolo high above the rest of the orchestra. This is pure parody, turning the soldier with his 'musket, fife, and drum' into a comic figure with a pathetic swagger in his march.

After a development which at moments takes the music more seriously, the movement runs to an exuberant close.

## 2nd movement: moderato

The slow movement starts with a lament on the clarinet.

Example 4

This leads to a duo with a second clarinet, and then a trio, with the flute joining in. A woodwind passage ensues, with the flute and oboe punctuated by stabs on the bassoon. As this passage dies, a shadowy figure on the muted strings winds its way uncertainly upwards. Horns enter, and the strings sound even more emaciated as they climb to frozen heights. One can think of this movement expressing the tragic cost of war; the mock heroics of the first movement leading to this sad reflection of their consequences in the cemetery.

## 3rd movement: presto

After this brief respite, we are plunged anew into the headlong pace of the opening. Clarinets, punctuated by bassoons, ripple out a rising and dipping theme, which is taken up by the rest of the wind section. Then, after a prolonged drum roll, the brass, very reticent until now, joins in, and a fiercely exultant trumpet solo holds sway above the seething orchestra. The opening refrain is heard twice more, and then linked to the *largo* which follows.

## 4th movement: largo

A declamation by tubas and trombones sounds very 'Russian' in orchestral colouring, and could almost be a passage from Tchaikovsky. Then a bassoon solo enters mournfully, with a telling effect. It is almost as if, at some solemn State ceremony, when the high and mighty of the land assemble to lay wreaths to the memory of the dead, a lone mourner breaks through the serried ranks of officials, and seeks to place his own wreath, and express a private grief.

## 5th movement: allegretto

The final note of the largo becomes the first note of the final movement, as the bassoon launches into a mocking tune. Some Soviet critics took great exception to the burlesque character of this movement, calling it 'grotesque', and 'a mockery of the listener'. But again, what Shostakovich is mocking is militarism itself. This is made clear, when, after a shadowy passage with sinister oboes and funereal horns, the mock victory march is thundered out by the whole orchestra.

# *Great interpreters*

Decca International

## Walter Weller (conductor)

Weller was born in Vienna in 1939, and studied at the Vienna Academy of Music. In 1956, while still a teenager, he joined the violins of the Vienna Philharmonic, and made sufficient progress and impact to enable him to form the Weller String Quartet two years later. This group toured extensively and successfully, as well as making several worthy records of chamber music for Decca in the late fifties. In 1961 he became leader of the Vienna Philharmonic, retaining that position until 1969.

His debut came with the Vienna Philharmonic in 1966 when he substituted for an ill Karl Böhm at short notice: soon after, a similar substitution for Krips with the Vienna Symphony confirmed the excellent impression he had already made, and his conducting career was under way: within a short time he was guest conducting on contract for the Vienna State Opera and the Volksoper. By 1971/2 he had positions as Musical Director at Duisurg and Niederösterreichisches Tonkünstler Orchestra, and the third Viennese Orchestra.

He has since been guest conductor for most of the top-line European orchestras, appearing frequently with the London Philharmonic Orchestra and the London Symphony Orchestra both in concert and on record. In 1976 he became Principal Conductor and Artistic Adviser to the Royal Liverpool Philharmonic in succession to Sir Charles Groves. From 1980 to 1985 he was Principal Conductor with the Royal Philharmonic Orchestra. Since then, he has been active as a guest conductor.

Weller's reputation is founded on the Central European tradition, especially in opera. On record his greatest achievements have tended to lie in his renditions of 20th-century composers such as Prokofiev, Rachmaninov and Britten.

---

### FURTHER LISTENING

**Shostakovich: Symphony No. 5**
Termed 'a Soviet artist's reply to just criticism', this rightfully famous symphony is a towering achievement, bordering on the Mahlerian in scope and emotional intensity. From the first abrupt and arresting phrases of the moderato the listener is aware of the gravity with which Shostakovich is approaching his task here, in attempting to construct a tightly-organized work of sufficient intellectual and emotional conviction to disarm his critics. After the gravity of the moderato and the almost unbearable intensity of the lyrical largo, it is a tribute to his genius that Shostakovich manages a completely convincing finale, unifying themes from all parts of the work.

**Shostakovich: The String Quartets**
Although he came late to the form – he wrote his first quartet in 1935, after having completed four symphonies – Shostakovich went on to write 15 quartets, creating a body of work which, along with Bartók's, stands as this century's supreme contribution to the quartet form. As Shostakovich approached old age, the quartets can be seen as an intimate artistic addressing of the problems of mortality: and the honesty which he brought to his task makes rewarding listening.

**Prokofiev: Piano Concerto No. 3**
Prokofiev's eventful life, moving from country to country, produced a steady series of masterpieces in virtually every musical form. Symphonies, concertos, operas and ballets – as well as the wonderful *Peter & The Wolf* – flowed from his pen, and he often said he was happy only when creating. The third Piano Concerto is a particularly outstanding orchestral achievement from his American period, displaying as it does so many characteristic Prokofievian traits such as harmonic violence and strength. It is unmistakably music of its time, immediately Russian in flavour, and yet has the timeless quality of all great music.

## IN THE BACKGROUND

# *'The Mad Monk'*

*The rise of Rasputin, the peasant 'holy man' who enthralled the Tsar and Tsarina of Russia, took him to such heights that, when he fell, Russia fell too — into the waiting hands of Revolution.*

*The Russian Royal Family – the Romanovs (left) – pictured in a satirical cartoon of the time, held in the grip of their monstrous protegé, Rasputin. This association, in combination with war and civil discontent, was to sink the Romanov dynasty and plunge all Russia into a sea of revolutionary blood.*

On 1 November 1905 Tsar Nicholas II of Russia made a simple entry in his diary: 'We've made the acquaintance of a man of God, Grigory from the province of Tobolsk.' The entry marks the beginning of a fateful relationship between the Royal House of Romanov and Grigory Rasputin. This particular man of God was to exert such a catastrophic influence over Russia's last royal family that it ultimately led to his murder, their murder and, some would say, to the Russian Revolution of 1917.

Grigory Rasputin was born in about 1872, in a Siberian village, the son of a horse farmer. He grew up a peasant, renowned for his remarkable strength. He was credited with second sight, and a capacity for predicting natural disasters. He was also an inveterate womanizer.

Some time in the early 1890s, after seeing a 'vision' of the Virgin Mary, Rasputin set off on his travels and so began his career as a wandering 'starets', an unordained holy man — a familiar character in pre-revolutionary Russia.

Soon after arriving in Petersburg in 1903, Rasputin acquired a considerable following of devoted admirers. The city was full of bored and credulous noblewomen who loved to dabble in spiritualism and the occult. Aristocratic women found him both mesmerizing and titillating, for he preached a doctrine of salvation through sin — especially sins of the flesh. Needless to say, he was happy to 'save' many of his female clients.

He made a conspicuous figure in St Petersburg, with his exotic peasant clothes, his unkempt hair and wild demeanour. Most striking of all were his 'magnetic eyes' with their curious sparkle and apparent ability to read another's innermost thoughts. It was this hypnotic power that endeared Rasputin to the Tsarina Alexandra. It was through hypnosis that 'Our Friend', as she always called Rasputin, was able to stem the haemorrhages that regularly threatened the life of the little heir to the throne, the Tsarevich, Alexii.

Since the day they discovered that their son, the Tsarevich, was a haemophiliac, Nicholas and Alexandra had been forced to watch him writhe in agony when minor injuries turned into great painful swellings. Medical science could do little to help. Today, it is possible to see how Rasputin's 'healing' could have worked. There is evidence that emotional

*Despite his extraordinary, depraved behaviour, Grigory Rasputin, under the protection of Tsarina Alexandra, became the darling of the salons (right). Using his almost magical 'charms' he cut swathes through the chastity of St Petersburg's society women — and absolved them of their sin afterwards.*

*The Romanov Summer Palace (left) at Tsarskoe Selo near St Petersburg, offered the Tsar and Tsarina the privacy they craved. Rasputin's influence rested in his ability to allay some of the worst effects of haemophilia – a disease afflicting their son and heir (above).*

stress aggravates haemorrhaging, while emotional stability can reduce it – even stem it altogether. However he did it, Rasputin's way with the Tsarevich seemed nothing short of miraculous to the Tsarina. For her he was a saint. Unfortunately, few of Alexandra's subjects understood. The Tsarevich's affliction was a closely guarded secret. And outsiders got a different view of the 'holy' Rasputin.

### Nicholas and Alexandra

The Tsarina's devotion to Rasputin was all-important in his rise to power, for she completely dominated her weak-willed husband. Unlike many dynastic marriages, theirs had been a love match and Nicholas worshipped his 'darling, adorable Alix'.

Four years younger than Nicholas, Alix was a grand-daughter of Queen Victoria and had been given a Victorian gentlewoman's education in London. Blue-eyed and fair-haired, she was the picture of a fairy-tale princess. But she possessed a will of iron and an intensely passionate nature. Having reluctantly relinquished her Protestantism in order to marry Nicholas, she embraced Russian Orthodoxy with the fanatical zeal of the convert. But neither bride nor groom was equipped to play their allotted roles as heads of state.

Unlike his father, Nicholas was timid and afraid of his authority. And Alexandra could not stand the round of elaborate court occasions demanded of heads of state. She quickly earned unpopularity for seeking privacy – she even drew the blinds on the imperial train when it came to a halt so that she would not have to face the gaze of the adoring people. A 'small family circle' was what Alexandra wanted. And Nicholas, whom Rasputin once graphic- ally described as 'a man without insides', submitted in everything to his passionate, forceful wife.

### Longing for an heir

Russia needed a male heir to the throne. But year after year Alexandra had produced daughters: Olga (1895), Tatiana (1897), Maria (1899) and Anastasia (1901). Each time her labour commenced, St Peters- burg listened for the 300-gun salute that would announce the birth of a tsarevich – the heir to the throne. But each time, the salute ceased after the 101st cannon had fired. In her bitter disappointment Alexandra became a natural quarry for any 'quack' who claimed to be able to change her fate. Consequently, a procession of dubious priests, astrologers, herbalists, spiritualists and faith healers found their way to Tsarskoe Selo, the palace outside St Petersburg, where Alexandra spent most of her time. It was with tremendous relief, therefore, that she finally gave birth to a son, Alexii, in 1904.

But the baby had inherited from his mother the curse which beset so many European royal families: haemophilia. After the birth of her son, Alexandra retreated even deeper into a private world in which only her family and the likes of Rasputin were welcome.

### The changing face of Russia

A Romanov emperor was the absolute ruler of 130 million people, 8.75 million square miles of territory. If Nicholas had been sensible enough to see how times were changing, he might have opted for constitutional monarchy instead of maintaining the traditional autocracy of the Tsars. But Nicholas, a shy, slight man, seemed happy to keep up the traditions of his huge, unyielding, autocratic and overbearing father, Alexander III.

With the help of repressive legislation and a massive policing system, Alexander had maintained the political status quo in Russia. But economically

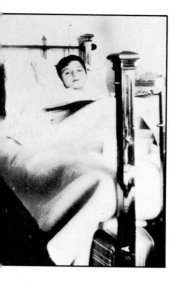

*The calamitous war of 1905 with Japan (below) was finally lost at sea. The disappointment was acute for Nicholas, yet he learned nothing of the need to modernize his armed forces nor the importance of competent, professional commanders.*

the face of Russia had changed and some kind of political change was inevitable – sooner or later.

Under a finance minister of genius, Sergei Witte, the process of modernizing the industrially backward country had begun. By the late 1880s trade was growing on a colossal scale; foreign capital began to flow in and a whole new range of industries sprang up around the principal cities. In the Donets Basin a new mining industry attracted peasant workers in their thousands, and Siberia was being colonized rather like the American 'Wild West'. In 1891 the Trans-Siberian Railway was begun – a massive undertaking that would link China with Europe and open up vast new markets.

But this belated industrial revolution was achieved at great social cost. The new proletariat suffered every kind of exploitation. Most remained illiterate and only a fraction ever received medical attention. While workers sweated in the industrial cities, the peasants subsisted on the land, always vulnerable to famine.

Conditions such as these gave rise to a many-sided revolutionary movement committed to trying to change the plight of the people. And opposition to the 'blind' autocracy of the tsar came from many different groups – the peasants, the urban workers, even the sons and daughters of the gentry. But it was the urban proletariat that eventually became the driving force towards revolution. Adopting Marxism as their political philosophy, the Social Democratic Party, founded in 1898, became committed to the industrial path to change. From these roots, the Bolsheviks the radical Communist Party faction,

emerged in 1903 to take the lead.

Earlier revolutionary movement had been forced underground and into terrorist strategies by Tsar Alexander III, but their growth during Nicholas' reign meant that they could not be suppressed indefinitely. Sensible observers therefore tried to make Tsar Nicholas take the initiative to forestall a revolution. In 1902, for example, the great novelist Tolstoy wrote to Nicholas urging him to introduce a form of democracy.

*I do not want to die without having told you what great good you are capable of bringing to yourself and millions of people, and what great evil you will bring to yourself and to millions if you continue on your present course.*

### The year of nightmares

The path to revolution began in earnest in 1905 (the very year in which Nicholas first met Rasputin) following the disastrous Russian-Japanese War that began in 1904.

Russia had been on the brink of war with Japan for several years over conflicting interest in the East. After the British lost their primacy in China with the Boxer Rebellion of 1900, several countries took the opportunity to move into China themselves. Eventually, Russia and Japan found themselves eye to eye in Korea, and war was declared.

The 18 months of hostilities that followed amounted to a catalogue of humiliations for Russia, culminating in the annihilation of the Russian fleet at Tsushima. Nicholas saw his undersupplied army and navy out-manoeuvred by an enemy he had harshly

referred to as 'little short-tailed monkeys'. Instead of enjoying the 'successful little war' he had expected, he lost in prestige, in damage to the morale of the imperial armed forces, and in the end to Russian dreams of expansion in the East.

Worst of all, the privations caused by the war aggravated the rising tide of discontent at home. 1905 – called by the Tsarina the 'year of nightmares' – began with the tragedy of Bloody Sunday – an atrocity for which Nicholas was blamed.

The hard-pressed workers of St Petersburg decided to make a direct appeal to the Tsar to improve their lot. A priest, Father Gapon, organized a mass demonstration outside the Winter Palace, to present Nicholas with a petition requesting an eight-hour day, a minimum wage of one rouble a day, and a parliamentary assembly.

The protest march was very respectable: even the tone of the petition was respectful rather than angry: 'We the workers of St Petersburg, our wives, children and helpless old folk, have come to you to seek justice and protection.' The workers – whole families – arrived in their Sunday best, looking purposeful but sober-minded. As they converged on the Winter Palace they sang hymns and carried portraits of Nicholas and Alexandra as well as icons.

Something akin to blind panic seized the military officers and the police, who had been told to 'deal with the situation'. (Nicholas was not even inside the Winter Palace, but at Tsarskoe Selo, about 15 miles away.) They called on the crowd to stop advancing and disperse. But there were too many people to be easily dispersed, and the marchers were in an exalted mood, convinced that they were about to meet the Tsar. They believed that their 'little father' had only to hear their grievances to do something! But as the crowd continued to move towards the palace, the soldiers opened fire – straight into the screaming, struggling mass of people. Then mounted cossacks charged after the unarmed civilians, cutting them down with sabres. More than 500 people were killed and several thousand wounded. The faith of many ordinary people in Tsar Nicholas died.

The atrocity provoked one of the most widespread general strikes Europe had ever known. By June, after the crushing defeat at Tsushima, there was a mutiny on the battleship Potemkin. Worker committees *(soviets)* were set up in St Petersburg factories.

Simultaneously, anti-Semitic pogroms added to the atmosphere of bloody revolt. Some were organized by the authorities, to deflect public anger away from the government. Prokofiev was a student at the St Petersburg Conservatory during this year and, during the unrest, Rimsky Korsakov was dismissed from his conservatory post.

Nicholas's first instinct was to call out the military and crush the strikes and disturbances. But Witte persuaded him to temper savage reprisals with a concession to reform. He issued a manifesto granting Russia the first constitution in its history and its first parliament, the Duma.

### The Dumas

The Duma, with its tiny electorate and few powers, aroused great hopes. But nothing had really changed in Nicholas's mind, and he entered 1906 determined to take back at the earliest opportunity the little power he had parted with. He could never forgive his people for their transgressions. He regarded the Duma deputies as seditious men of evil intent,

P. Kotov 'Barricades at Gorbatov Bridge' Novosti

though most of them were in fact quite conservative.

The first two Dumas proved to be bitter, unworkable experiments in constitutional government. Nicholas dissolved the first after only two months and, although three more were elected before 1914, they wielded little power. Unfortunately, the man who could have forged a workable partnership between Tsar and Duma, Peter Stolypin, fell victim to an assassin in 1911.

Peter Stolypin was no liberal, but he opposed every one of the Tsar's efforts to suppress the Duma. And he was able to initiate a massive programme of agrarian reform. He also tried to do something about Rasputin, whose intimacy with the Tsarina and her daughters now gave rise to the most lurid rumours.

The Tsarina's pet holy man was given to the most outrageous public behaviour (though he conducted himself with sober decorum at the palace). On the grounds of police reports itemizing Rasputin's drunken assignations with innumerable women, and his boasts of influence over the Tsarina, Stolypin attempted to have him sent back to Siberia. But to no avail. The Tsarina was furious, and saw Stolypin's assassination as an act of divine retribution: 'Those who have offended God in the person of Our Friend may no longer count on divine protection.'

Stolypin's successor broached the subject of Rasputin's influence with the Tsarina. But even Maria Feodorovna, the dowager Tsarina, felt powerless to intervene. 'My unhappy daughter-in-law does not realize that she is destroying not only herself but the dynasty as well.' Not only was Rasputin a saint for Alexandra, he was also an embodiment of 'the people'. She felt herself a stranger in a hostile country, and loathed the politicians in the Duma. Rasputin represented what she imagined to be the strength and affectionate honesty of the Russian peasant. He related to her and her family casually, and gave the impression of liking them as human beings. It was easy to believe that 'out there', in the countryside, the Tsar's subjects shared Rasputin's simple sense of loyalty – it was only at court and in the corrupt cities that they were disliked and criticized. As the criticism mounted, Rasputin's influence grew until, when war broke out in 1914, he found himself in a powerful position.

### World War

There had been such an air of imminent doom that many people felt a sense of relief at the declaration of War. And just as he had welcomed the Russo-Japanese War, Nicholas hoped that the war effort

*Prime Minister Stolypin (below) worked unstintingly to protect the Duma (bottom). He also tried to expose Rasputin's vices to the Tsarina, but to no avail. He was assassinated in 1911.*

*Bloody Sunday – the massacre of peaceful demonstrators outside the Winter Palace in 1905 shook the proletariat out of its docile devotion to the Tsar. The scene is immortalized in the classic Russian film The Battleship Potemkin (above) as the true starting point of the Great Revolution of 1917. Strikes and riots followed 'Bloody Sunday' and barricades went up in the streets (left). Nicholas was obliged by it to concede a token representation of the people – the Duma – Russia's first elected parliament.*

Popperfoto

Popperfoto

*In his capacity as Commander in Chief, Nicholas (left, blessing his troops) sent a million men into battle in World War 1 with insufficient clothing, food or arms. A stream of 'communiques' from his wife passed on to him Rasputin's ideas on handling the War. Rasputin, in effect, ruled while Nicholas was at the Front.*

would rally the country around him. This was a fantasy: the army had been left in such incompetent hands since the 1904–5 fiasco that after less than a week of fighting in 1914 it had run out of ammunition. Within a month there were disastrous and massive defeats at Tannenburg and the Massurian Lakes.

Nicholas delighted in army life far more than in handling the day-to-day affairs of state in St Petersburg. He was tempted to go to the front as Commander-in-Chief, and his wife encouraged him.

The war aroused Alexandra to a blaze of patriotic and religious activity and her strategy was simple. Nicholas must go to the front to lead his troops to victory personally. The Duma must be crushed. She, with the help of Rasputin would take over the reins of government. The cabinet protested, but their protests were brushed aside. The Duma protested, so the Duma was suspended. In effect, Rasputin was virtually ruler of Russia and he ushered in a series of government dismissals and reshuffles, intrigues and conspiracies. This situation, combined with defeat after defeat at the front, brought the country, once again, to the brink of revolution.

Rasputin attached great significance to his dreams, and on the strength of them sent orders to the Tsar. Nicholas was even advised to comb his hair with Rasputin's comb before making any major decisions. Alexandra kept up a barrage of 'inspired' advice. A typical communication (1916) read: 'Our Friend begs you not to worry too much about this question of food supply – says things will arrange themselves.'

Still Rasputin encouraged the Tsarina in her ill-judged attempt to keep Russia an absolute monarchy for 'Baby and Nicky'. Anyone holding office who showed the least efficiency, honesty or initiative was dismissed. Reliable ministers were replaced with grotesquely unsuitable candidates – such as Protopopov to whom the Ministry of the Interior was given. This admirer of Rasputin's, this dabbler in the occult, was afflicted with a chronic disease, probably syphilis, and was half mad. Even Nicholas felt constrained to say, 'Our Friend's opinions of people are sometimes very strange.' The situation had developed into a nightmare. A group of determined men decided to kill Rasputin.

### The assassination of Rasputin

Rasputin's murderers were not revolutionaries or even liberal reformers. They were all monarchists, blue-blooded aristocrats or conservative politicians,

who saw the removal of this charlatan as the only way of saving the Tsar. Some hoped that, after the death, Alexandra would be removed to a mental home and that Nicholas would then resume his place at the head of the nation. They laid their plans carefully, for though they felt contempt for Rasputin, he still frightened them. The 'bait' was to be a woman – none other than the beautiful Princess Irina, niece of the Tsar and wife of Prince Yusupov, one of the conspirators. Rasputin was told that she desired a private meeting with him.

Downstairs at his palace, Prince Yusupov pre-

*A German cartoon of 1915 (above) likens the soldier-Tsar to Shakespeare's Macbeth – knee-deep in the blood of his own people, spilt by blindly pursuing his own misguided ambitions.*

pared a special 'murder chamber' furnished with antiques, a white bearskin rug, costly Persian carpets and a crucifix to neutralize Rasputin's diabolic powers. On a table were little cakes laced with cyanide, and bottles of poisoned wines which it was hoped would tempt Rasputin. On 29 December 1916, Prince Yusupov went by car to collect Rasputin from his apartment and bring him to the palace. It was midnight and Rasputin was eager, all dressed in his best. His hair was slicked down with oil, his beard was trimmed, he wore a white silk blouse and black velvet trousers, and he smelled strongly of cheap soap. Escorted to the chamber, he was told that the Princess was detained by visitors, but that she would be down shortly. The other conspirators were gathered upstairs and made 'sociable' noises so as to sound like guests, and played over and over again a phonograph of *Yankee Doodle.*

To Yusupov's frustration, Rasputin refused to eat or drink anything at first. Then, when he did, he showed no ill-effects: he even suggested that the Prince play gypsy songs on a guitar! While the Prince sang, the 'victim' thrived, and at two-thirty in the morning Yusupov, who could stand the strain no longer, went upstairs to fetch a revolver.

Meanwhile, Rasputin did not appear to be well – he was drooping and breathing heavily. But another glass of poisoned wine 'revived' him, and he proposed – since there was no sign of the Princess – an outing to a gypsy establishment, 'with God in thought but with mankind in flesh'. Yusupov then suggested that Rasputin should say a prayer in front of the crucifix. As Rasputin knelt Yusupov shot him. Rasputin fell backwards on to the rug, and the other conspirators came tumbling into the room. Casting a final glance at the 'corpse', Yusupov was horrified to see one eye still twitching. At the same moment Rasputin grasped him by the shoulder and tore off one of his epaulettes. Then he staggered to his feet and, 'roaring with fury', managed to reach a side door of the palace and the small yard outside it. Just as he was about to reach the gate on to the street, another of the conspirators shot him again. Yusupov, hysterical by now, battered the body with a steel press just to be sure . . . yet still Rasputin lived – one

of his eyes was still open. The conspirators then tied his hands together, wrapped his body in a blue curtain, and dumped it through a hole in the ice of the River Neva. In their haste they left one of his fur boots behind on the ice, helping the police in their search for the body. When he was found, Rasputin had indeed managed to free himself of the rope and his lungs were full of water, proving that he had not been dead when dropped into the icy water.

## Murder and revolution
A few days later the news of Rasputin's death was all over St Petersburg, and the murderers, whose identities were common knowledge, were regarded as heroes. So despite the Tsarina's distress, they were dealt with leniently: Prince Yusupov was simply banished to one of his country estates. Nicholas hurried back from the front to comfort Alexandra who had gone into a trance of mystical sorrow. Rasputin was buried, with the royal family as mourners, in the Imperial Park and, day by day, the Tsarina went to pray by her *staret's* tomb.

But the murderers' hope of shocking the Tsar into more responsible behaviour was fruitless. Nicholas shut himself up in Tsarskoe Selo with his family, ignoring signs of revolution. Rasputin had prophesied, 'While I live, your throne is secure. If I die, you will lose your throne and your life.'

By January 1917 there were daily strikes and protests in St Petersburg. The city was full of demoralized and disaffected soldiers waiting to be sent to the front. Those at the front did not even have enough rifles to go round. Experience gained in 1905 had prepared revolutionaries for this moment. Gloomy and apathetic, Nicholas ignored all advice to appease his people. By March he had been forced to abdicate in favour of a provisional government.

In November, the Bolsheviks under Lenin seized power from the provisional liberal government. Soon civil war raged between the 'Reds' (Bolsheviks) and the 'Whites' (anti-communists). In April 1918 the royal family was moved to Ekaterinburg in the Urals. There, Nicholas, Alexandra and their five children were executed by local Bolsheviks, as a pro-White Czech legion approached. The course was now set for Russia's communist future.

*The tide of revolution finally overtook the Romanovs. While rival revolutionaries fought for control in a bitter civil war, they were captured and held prisoners by the Bolsheviks. Left with no part to play in Russia's future the order for their execution (below) came as a matter of course. The photograph, below left, shows the family shortly before their imprisonment. They were shot, all together, in 1918.*

# Contemporary composers

## Alexander Dargomīzhsky (1813-1869)

Dargomīzhsky studied piano and violin during his youth in St. Petersburg. A friendship with Glinka in 1833 encouraged him to compose in earnest. During the following years he completed three operas, and in the 1860s began work on a fourth, based on Pushkin's play, *The Stone Guest.* In this work, he followed realist aims, seeking to match the musical lines exactly with the rise and fall of Russian speech patterns. This bold idea caught the attention of the Mighty Handful. Dargomīzhsky died in 1869 before finishing the opera, but Cui and Rimsky-Korsakov finished the score and the orchestration. The opera had its debut in 1872.

## Alexander Glazunov (1865-1936)

At sixteen, Alexander Glazunov had not only studied composition with Rimsky-Korsakov and earned the praise of Balakirev, but he had also premièred his *First Symphony* to wide acclaim. His early works were strongly influenced by the Russian nationalist movement; like many nationalists, he enhanced his compositions with folk melodies. Glazunov wrote ballets, concertos and seven more symphonies, continuing to explore melodic ideas while moving away from pure nationalism. He became director of the St. Petersburg Conservatory in 1906, while still composing small-scale works. He left the Soviet Union in 1928 to settle in the West; after a one-year tour of the United States, he moved to Paris, where he died in 1936.

## Reinhold Glière (1875-1956)

The son of a musician and instrument maker, Reinhold Glière studied music in his hometown of Kiev before entering the Moscow Conservatory. After graduating in 1900, he taught composition at the Conservatory and became interested in Russian folk music. He incorporated diverse national elements in his operas and ballets. His international reputation was greatly enhanced by his ballet, *The Red Poppy* (1927) and his *Harp Concerto* (1938). Although his later works were criticized for their political motivation, he continued to influence young composers, including his student Sergei Prokofiev. He died in Moscow in 1956.

## Mikhail Glinka (1804-1857)

The father of the Russian nationalist school and the first Russian composer to win international fame, Mikhail Glinka studied music in St. Petersburg and Berlin. His operas *A Life for the Tsar* (1836) and *Ruslan and Lyudmila* (1842) helped to establish a true Russian national style. *Ruslan and Lyudmila,* in particular, featured oriental themes later found in other nationalist music. He spent the following years abroad; in Paris, where his were the first Russian works performed in the West, and in Spain, where he wrote orchestral pieces based on Spanish folk tunes. Although his works were comparatively few, his influence on the styles of later composers was profound. He died in Berlin in 1857.

## Aram Khachaturian (1903-1978)

Of Armenian descent, Aram Khachaturian became known for his contributions toward a nationalist Armenian style. He studied music in Moscow and later became a professer at the Moscow Conservatory. Outside Russia, he was best known for his *Piano Concerto* (1936) and for his ballets *Spartacus* (1954) and *Gayane* (1942), which features the Sabre Dance. He also composed the Armenian national anthem, symphonies, concertos, and incidental music for films. In 1948, he was condemned, with Prokofiev and Shostakovich, by the Central Committee for writing bourgeois music, but after Stalin's death he returned to prominence. He died in 1978.

## Peter Ilyich Tchaikovsky (1840-1893)

The leading Russian composer of the late 19th century, Peter Ilyich Tchaikovsky is best remembered for his remarkable gifts of melody and orchestration. His ballet scores for *Swan Lake, Sleeping Beauty* and the *Nutcracker* have become classics. He studied music in St. Petersburg before accepting a teaching post at the Moscow Conservatory in 1866, the year his first symphony premièred. He composed prolifically over the next several years, at times hampered by long periods of depression. Though some of his music shared common links with the nationalist style, his works were above all highly personal. He toured Europe and America during the last few years of his life to wide acclaim. He died in St. Petersburg in 1893.

---

# Bibliography

Abraham, G. *The New Grove Russian Masters.* Norton (New York, 1986).

Bertensson, S. and J. Leyda. *Sergei Rachmaninov: A Lifetime in Music.* Da Capo (New York, 1970).

Guttman, D. *Prokofiev.* Seven Hill Books (Cincinatti, 1988).

Lukjanova, N. *Shostakovich.* Paganiniana (Neptune, 1984).

Norris, G. *Rachmaninov.* Littlefield (Totowa, 1978).

Ottaway, H. *Shostakovich Symphonies.* University of Washington Press (Seattle, 1978).

Roseberry, E. *Shostakovich: His Life and Times.* Hippocrene Books (New York, 1982).

Savkina. *Prokofiev.* Paganiniana (Neptune, 1984).

Samuel, C. *Prokofiev.*

Vienna House (New York, 1980).

Seroff, V. *Sergei Prokofiev: A Soviet Tragedy.* Taplinger (New York, 1979).

Schwarz, B. *Music and Musical Life in Soviet Russia 1917-70.* University of Indiana Press (Bloomington, 1978).

Threltall, R. and G. Norris. *A Catalog of the Compositions of S. Rachmaninov.* Gower Publishing (Brookfield, 1982).

Volvov, S., ed. *Testimony: The Memoirs of Dmitri Shostakovich.* Limelight Editions (New York, 1984).

# Index